BULLMASTIFFS
TODAY

Lyn Pratt

HOWELL
BOOK HOUSE
New York

This book is dedicated to the memory of our first Bullmastiff – Asliz Buttonoak (alias Kelly).

HOWELL BOOK HOUSE
A Simon & Schuster / Macmillan Company
1633 Broadway
New York, NY 10019

MACMILLAN is a registered trademark of Macmillan, Inc.

Library of Congress Cataloging-in-Publication data available on request.

ISBN 0–87605–064–X

Manufactured in Singapore

10 9 8 7 6 5 4 3 2

CONTENTS

Acknowledgements

Thanks are due to my niece, Freda Whittaker, for typing the manuscript, to her husband, Paul, for producing the line drawings, to Anne Kenman of Queensland, Australia, who provided material on Obedience and Training Targets, and to all those who supplied information and photographs for inclusion in the book.

LYN PRATT.

Chapter One

ORIGINS OF THE BULLMASTIFF

Where do we begin? What is a Bullmastiff? Some say that a Bullmastiff is the result of careful breeding between the Bulldog and the Mastiff. Others say that a Bullmastiff is a direct descendant of the Gamekeepers' Night Dog. Many of the pedigrees have been handed down without any thought as to their authenticity. For many dog owners, a copy of a pedigree containing noted bloodlines means more than the actual value of the dog.

The first Bullmastiffs registered at the Kennel Club were under the heading 'Foreign Dogs'. In May 1881 we find 'Nelson, d, Bull Mastiff, Mr A. F. Styles', by Scruncter – Lady. March 1879'. In July 1883 there is 'Brutus, d, bull-mastiff, Mr W. W. Brownjohn's (late Miss Chigwan's – pedigree unknown).' There is a slight difference, as the latter breed description carries small letters and the name is hyphenated. It is pertinent here to clarify the changes which took place in the breed name. In the Kennel Club records the name was hyphenated until August 1927. The registrations up to March 1939 inclusive were headed Bull Mastiffs. In April of the same year they were headed Bullmastiffs. In 1947 Clifford L. B. Hubbard wrote in his book *The Bullmastiff* that: "Originally the breed name was Bull Mastiff as two words and with no mistake about it. Personally I prefer this form, even today when I know in doing so I am with a lost cause. I have never until writing this book used the form 'Bullmastiff' on any occasion whatever in any of my writings concerning the breed, or in any of my classification tables. If you look back into the breed's history you will find there was, at first, only the one form, and then that awful hyphen crept in, with the result that eventually the trend was allowed undisciplined rein and sped, to its logical conclusion, to the single word coined from the original two." It can therefore be taken that the modern form is one word and where other forms appear in this book it is because the information is taken from documents pre-dating 1939.

When George R. Jesse produced his *Researches into the British Dog* in 1886, he included the following: "Prestwick Eaton wrote from St Sebastian to George Wellingham in St. Swithin's Lane, London in 1631 and 1632 for several things; amongst which he wanted 'a goode mastive dogge', his case of bottles 'replenyshed with best lickour' and 'pray procuer me two good bulldoggs and let them bee sent by ye first shipp'." Jesse goes on to describe the Bulldog: "It doubtless was originally a short nosed Mastiff as described by Houghton, and so bred, that his truncated muzzle and jaws might obtain a firmer grip, and prevent the bull from swinging him off." (This is a reference to the dog being used for bull-baiting.) Shakespeare mentions the mastiff often, but the bulldog never. In course of time a fancy arose for a smaller breed; perhaps owing to a desire to obtain the highest amount of courage united with the smallest amount of physical power – a sort of toy dog of the day; the most diminutive which could still pin a bull. The animal had degenerated greatly, the disgusting abortions exhibited at shows being deformities from foot to muzzle, mere

*These models
were made around
1790; the likeness
was taken from
two dogs living in
England. At that
time, the ears of
all fighting dogs
were cropped to
the skull to avoid
damage when in
combat.*

caricatures of the original race, and totally incapable of dealing with a veteran bull. An old work describes the bulldog as "somewhat smaller than a mastiff, but in form nearly allied to it; the body robust and the lips pendulous at the sides".

In Volume Two, Jesse included *The Whole Art of Husbandry*, first written by Conrade Heresbatch and translated by Barnaby Googe in 1631. It gives a good description of the Mastiff and also a species called the Bandog. "The Bandog for the House. First the Mastie that keepeth the house. For this purpose you must provide you such a one as hath a large and mightie body, a great and shrill voyce, that both with his barking he may discover, and with his sight dismay the theefe, yea, being not seene, with the horror of his voyce put him to flight. His stature must neither be long nor short, but well set; his head great; his eyes sharpe and fiery, either brown or grey; his lippes blackish, neither turning up, nor hanging too much downe; his mouth blacke and wide; his neather jawe fat, and coming out of it on either side a fang, appearing more outward than his other teeth; his upper teeth even with his neather, not hanging too much over, sharpe and hidden with his lippes; his countenance like a lion, his brest great and shaghayrd; his shoulders broad; his legges bigge; his tayle short; his feet very great; his disposition must neither be too gentle, not too curst, that he neither fawn upon a theefe, nor flee upon his friends; very waking; no gadder abroad, nor lavish of his mouth, barking without cause; neither maketh it any matter though he be not swift, for he is but to fight at home, and to give warning of the enimie." Jesse's own opinion of this translation followed: "Though this is taken from a foreign work, nevertheless, it is probable that the translation was a liberal one, and gave a tolerably correct portrait of our Mastiff, or rather Bull-Mastiff, and not a distinct, lighter and more active dog as represented by the incomparable Thomas Bewick."

In 1851 the Fifth Edition of Blaine's *Canine Pathology*, revised and corrected by Walton Mayer, was published and here is the section devoted to Mastiffs. "Canis Urcani – The Mastiffs. Muzzle truncated; cranium elevated; frontal sinus large; condyles of the lower jaw above the lines of the upper molars; mouth rounder in front; ears small, partially drooping; tail carried erect; structure powerful. Inhabited originally high mountain ranges and the more temperate regions of the northern hemisphere in the old continent."

Canis urcanus	The Mastiff of Tibet
Canis urcanus	The English Mastiff
Canis urcanus	The Cuba Mastiff
Canis Anglicus	The Bull-dog
Canis Anglicus	The Bull Terrier
Canis Anglicus	The Pug Dog
Canis fricator	The Roquet
Canis fricator	The little Danish Dog
Canis fricator	The Artois mongrel
Canis fricator	The Alicant Dog

'Dogs Baiting The Bulls': From a series of etchings titled 'La Tauromaquia' by Francisco de Goya. Courtesy: Christina de Lima Netto.

'The Horse Corral in the Old Madrid Bullring before a Fight' by Manuel Castellano, 1815. Note the Bullmastiff in the left hand corner. Courtesy: Christina de Lima Netto.

In 1872 the Second Edition of *The Dogs of the British Isles*, edited by "Stonehenge", was published. Here we find a reference to the Gamekeepers' Night Dog, by "Idstone". Many still believe that this was the origin of the Bullmastiff. "The Mastiff, or a Mastiff crossed with the Bloodhound, is the dog a keeper generally prefers; but the men have their own ideas on the subject, and generally know pretty well where to obtain a promising young dog from each other for a little money. As there is not much demand for them, those keepers who breed them seldom save more than a couple in a litter, and consequently they are for the most part vigorous examples, and large; indeed, power and a certain happy combination of ferocity and intelligence are the chief requisites in a night dog."

DOGS FOR INDIAN HUNTING

What has India got to do with the Bullmastiff, you may well ask? Well, 'Dogs for Indian Hunting' was the heading of an excerpt from Sanderson's *Elephant Catching in India*, and it was in the *Kennel Gazette* for April 1884. I do not propose to give you the whole of the excerpt here, but just enough to give you another picture of what could have been the original Bullmastiff. The author goes on at great length describing the various methods used to hunt jackals, the Indian fox, the large civet-cat, wild hogs, bears, panthers and bison. It is my intention to select relevant sections. "A pack for dangerous game hunting should comprise about three couples of seizers, and three or four couples of good terriers and crossbreeds for finding game and bringing it to bay for the operations of the seizers. These finding dogs should not be too small, otherwise they may not give tongue sufficiently loudly; and one or two should be fast. They should be plucky enough to keep in attendance on a beast, whatever demonstrations he makes against them, but not so courageous as to go at him.

"The seizers should be bulldogs or bull-mastiffs. In using the word bulldog I mean the dogs – usually bull and terrier – commonly termed bulldogs. The true breed is seldom large enough, and the true bull is a particularly unintelligent and peaceable animal. It is necessary to hit a happy medium. The bulldog's determined courage and forward attack must be joined with the terrier's vivacity and intelligence. With too much of the bull in his composition a dog will be stupid; whilst if the terrier element preponderates too strongly his courage may be doubtful, and, what is fatal in a seizer, he may go at some other part of the animal than the head.

"The first animals I introduced my pack to were a couple of bears. I had the following six seizers then:-
Marquis: an imported bull-mastiff weighing 40 lb.
Lady: a country-bred bull terrier bitch, 35 lb.
Bismark, Viper and Fury: pups of the above, weighing about 30 lb each, nine months old.
Turk: a country-bred bull terrier weighing 40 lb."

Marquis and Viper were sent in to attack a bear. "Marquis and Viper were more or less clawed, but not seriously. This bear weighed exactly 280 lb or 20 st." Could these small courageous dogs be the ancestors of the dogs we know today?

In 1892 the following story appeared in the *Kennel Gazette* but no mention was made of the writer's name. Although the story begins with a 'Bull-Mastiff' it ends with a 'Mastiff'. "An exciting fight has been witnessed between a Bull-Mastiff and a snake about four feet five inches long in Entally, India. The gentleman in whose house the occurrence took place keeps a large poultry-yard, and the snake, intending no doubt to make a meal of one of the fowl or ducks, was stealthily crawling into the yard, when the birds, scenting an enemy, began to cackle and flutter about in their alarm. The snake had just caught a duck, when the Bull-Mastiff came running to the spot, attracted by the noise, sprang upon the snake, and seized it close to the head. Acting on the defensive now, the snake released the duck, and, coiling itself round its antagonist, endeavoured to crush it. It compelled the dog to roll over; but the latter refused to quit his hold, while with his hind paws he struggled to tear the coils off him. This he partly succeeded in doing, and regained his feet; but the reptile once more coiled round him, and it appeared now as if the dog could be strangled, the folds of the snake forming a double ring round the Mastiff's neck." (Note change of name here). "The wriggling of the snake and the frantic struggles of the dog were now terrible to witness, and were all the more intensely watched from the fact that no help could be rendered to the plucky dog who never relaxed his grip. Both combatants rolled over a second time, and continued struggling for fully five minutes, while the dog pawed up the ground all round, and at last managed to make a slit in the skin of the snake by means of his claws. This was the beginning of the end. The dog once more threw off the coils, and rose to his feet. Releasing his grip for moment, he made a dash at the head of the snake and completely crushed it. Having disabled the snake so far, he tore the snake's body till the reptile was disembowelled. After a severe contest, extending over quarter of an hour, the dog gained a complete victory. Strange to relate, the Mastiff, with the exception of a large swelling in the inside of his mouth, sustained no injury."

Was it a Bull-Mastiff or a Mastiff? Was it fact or fiction? A good story gains a little in the telling. Does this story help us to discover how, when and where today's Bullmastiff was evolved?

THE MASTIFFS AND BULLDOGS OF THE LATE 19th CENTURY

Returning from India we must look at events in Britain. Forgetting about the Gamekeepers' Night Dog we can concentrate on the two breeds from whence the Bullmastiff derived its name. Kennel Club Stud Books were in existence before the *Kennel Gazettes*. In No. 1 Volume 1 of the *Kennel Gazette* published in April 1880 the following announcement was made: "Kennel Club Registry of Names: Copy of Rule. Every dog exhibited at a show held under the Kennel Club rules must, previous to the time of entry for such show, be in a registry of names kept by the Kennel Club at their office, 29a Pall Mall, London, SW. A charge of one shilling each dog will be made for registration. A name that has been already assumed and duly registered in the Kennel Club Registry, or entered in any published number of the Kennel Club Calendar and Stud Book, by the owner of a dog of the same breed, cannot be registered unless by a distinguishing name or number. Dogs that are already entered in any published number of the Kennel Club Calendar and Stud Book are exempt from the above rule, provided their names remain unchanged." If my arithmetic is correct, earlier Kennel Club Stud Books were published from 1873 to 1879. My records cover most of the *Kennel Gazettes* from 1880 and the Kennel Club Stud Books from 1929. In the first group of names registered in April 1880 there were twelve Mastiffs and eleven Bulldogs.

There must have been two Mastiffs by name of Prince, the first being distinguished by a number – 6357. The same thing occurred in Bulldogs where there were two by the name of Crib, the first being distinguished by the number 8558. This must have caused many problems with extended pedigrees. In the same issue there was a section for Stud Dogs in which eight Mastiffs and two Bulldogs were entered. In the stud dog section, weight and colours were given. In Mastiffs there were six fawns, one dark brindle and one rich fallow. The weights went from 140 lbs to 180 lbs. The two Bulldogs were a fawn and a brindle and weighed 48 lbs and 55 lbs. During the following months of 1880 weights in the Mastiffs varied between 140 and 180 lbs but new colours came in – stone, fawn and smutty fawn. Bulldogs remained the same. In 1881 three new colours came up in Mastiffs – fallow with intense black muzzle; fawn/black points; fawn light muzzle. The surprise was to see two Neros – Nero 9334, fawn/black points; 205 lbs. Nero 6378, fawn 178 lbs. In the same year Bulldogs came up with different colours and weights. Two were registered as white and one as fallow pied. One of the white Bulldogs weighed only 23 lbs and the fallow pied weighed

100 lbs. With such a variation in weight and colour some breeders began to complain about crosses between the two breeds. In a letter to the editor of the *Kennel Gazette,* published in January 1882, H. Smith (one-time secretary to the Bull Dog Club) wrote: "In a great many Bulldogs there is clear evidence of the Mastiff cross for size, or the Pug dog cross for body and darkness of muzzle and, as a general rule, I, and others who have bred the Bulldog for nearly half a century, also am of the opinion that very great care should be exercised before giving any award to a fallow, fallow-pied, or fawn coloured so-called Bulldog, as those tints are decidedly not pure Bulldog colour, which is white or brindle, or white and brindle." In February 1885 a judge of Mastiffs, Lt. Col. Garnier was criticising the Mastiffs because he said that some of them were showing signs of Bulldog influence: "I believe the Bulldog cross which has been used to be most useful for improving the breed, on the same principle as it has improved the Greyhound, but the cross should have been sufficiently bred out so as to leave all Mastiff characteristics unimpaired, whereas the exact contrary has been done."

In October of the same year "John Bull" writes a lengthy article about "The Weight of Bulldogs". His final paragraph is very interesting because it poses problems which are with us today. "To dub a dog a Bull-Mastiff, because he weighs over 60 lbs, is absurd; but the appearance of most of the specimens exhibited is certainly some excuse for the harsh accusation. It by no means follows that because a dog and a bitch are large that they will breed large stock, or vice versa, and in the same litter size will vary greatly. In one litter of three, all of them well-known prize winners, the weights at fifteen months were 62 lb, 37 lb and 31 lb."

Twelve years later we see a mention of the Bull Mastiff. W. R. H. Temple was giving his opinion of the "Foreign Dogs" exhibited in 1896. "I do not presume to be a judge of the Dogue de Bordeaux, and, as I have said before, if an Englishman wants an utterly hideous, dangerous brute, he can rig himself up in his own country with a Bull-Mastiff, without going across the Channel to find the article." This critique brought a response from an unnamed writer who described another dog. "The fact is, there is an island of the name of Terceira, whereon dwells various breeds of dog, but of these breeds that which preponderates is the yellowish-brown Bulldog – a dog which is abundant in that island, and the characteristic dog of the place. This dog, which is of the colour described, often possesses a black face, stands about two feet high, and whilst sometimes gentle it is frequently a very savage and dangerous animal. The ears are usually cropped, and the short, deformed tail is docked to a stub."

The judge for Dogues de Bordeaux at the Kennel Clubs Show in 1897 was G. R. Krehl and here is his opinion of that breed. "Club members and owners after the judging thanked me for having fixed the type by my awards. My selections were based upon my personal knowledge and study of the breed, and I went for a type that only the wilfully blind or hopelessly ignorant could say were overgrown Bulldogs or stunted Mastiffs." When R. G. S. Mann reviewed the Dogues de Bordeaux at the end of 1897 he wrote: "There is no doubt that ten or fifteen years ago certain French fanciers did use the English Mastiff for the purpose of adding to their dogs' stature and though the cross does not seem to have had any very serious results, except in a few kennels, yet one Dogue who almost certainly had this taint in his blood was shown in England soon after the breed was first introduced here, and some others have appeared on the benches since. This gave a slight colour to the Bull-Mastiff theory." What was the Bull-Mastiff theory? Although little was known of the Bull-Mastiff at this time, it was apparent that some people thought the breed was crossed with the imported Dogues de Bordeaux.

In January 1899 W. R. H. Temple must have been very pleased to write the following: "The Dogue de Bordeaux seems to have had a short and merry life before the public, for at the last Chow and Foreign Dog Show the classes provided for him were marked 'No Entry', R I P."

Although the Dogue de Bordeaux Club ceased to exist and there were no further breed classes, the blood lines were here. Were they included in the formation of the Bullmastiff? Dr J. Sydney Turner judged Mastiffs at the Birmingham Show in November 1889 and in his general preamble he said: "It would be a pity indeed if this true British dog should ever be allowed to die out. It could never be revived, because it is not an intermediate breed, but it is at the extreme end of the scale; a giver of type to many other breeds, but receiving none back, if we except the other British dog – the Bulldog. In my opinion, however, the Bulldog is more likely to be a small Mastiff than the Mastiff to be a large Bulldog." Dr Turner's words must be given some credence, as he was one of the founder members of the Old English Mastiff Club and from 1886-1908 he was the President of the Club.

MASTIFFS AND BULL-MASTIFFS OF THE EARLY 20th CENTURY

The few books which have been written on the Bullmastiff all give mention of Thorneywood Terror, said to be the greatest Night Dog ever bred. He was a small brindle, owned by Mr W. Burton of Thorneywood, Nottingham. Burton gave many demonstrations with his dog, where challengers were offered prize money if they could stand up against Terror, who was always muzzled. Classes were put on for Gamekeepers' Night Dogs for the first time in July 31st, August 1st and 2nd 1900 at the Royal Aquarium (Gamekeepers' Show). W. Burton was the judge. Only two dogs were mentioned – Working 2, W. Rooker's Wroxton Jim. Typical 2, W Rooker's Wroxton Jim; 3, J Cowell's Venius. No further mention was made of these dogs. In 1901 W. Burton again judged the classes at Crystal Palace, but there was no report; nor was there any report for 1902.

In 1903 The Gamekeepers' Annual Dog Show was held in conjunction with the Derby Show, July 22nd and 23rd. No mention was made of the judge, only the placings: Gamekeepers' Night Dogs – 1. R. Dye's Gotham Lion; 2. Fox's Clifton Terror; 3. H. Butcher's Saxondale Nellie. In the Mastiff registrations for August 1903 there are two bitches and one dog, all sired by Thorneywood Terror: Allestree Judy, b, Mr W. Arnold, sired by Mr Burton's Thorneywood Terror out of Mrs Hill's Fury III, August 1902. Clifton Hall, b, and Clifton Terror, d, Mr J. Fox, sired by Mr W. Burton's Thorneywood Terror out of owner's Clifton Lass, May 1st 1902. I have been unable to find the registration of Thorneywood Terror but in the Mastiffs for August 1901 we find Clifton Lass, b, Mr J. Fox, sired by Mr F. Martin's Burke out of Mr W. Burton's Vicious, March 25th 1894. Was Thorneywood Terror a pure-bred Mastiff? Was Clifton Lass eight years old when she whelped Clifton Hall and Clifton Terror? Gotham Lion was also registered as a Mastiff in September 1903. He was by Mr L. Linkley's Tiger out of owner's Ratcliffe Furie, October 18th 1901.

July 1905 sees another Mastiff bitch registration – Mr W. Blackburn's Ratcher Hill Bessie, who was litter sister to Clifton Hall and Clifton Terror. March 1906 sees Thorneywood Tinker, d, Mr W. Burton, sired by owner's Thorneywood Terror out of his Thorneywood Duchess, April 1902. May of the same year and we see Boy, d, Mr W. G. Grimble, sired by Mr W. Burton's Thorneywood Terror out of Mr J. H. Biggs' Osmaston Nell, February 7th 1905. All the dogs and bitches mentioned so far have been registered as Mastiffs. In June 1908 in the section headed Cross Breeds there is one entry – Bull Mastiff. Prince, d, Mr N. Richard, by Thorneywood Terror, dam unknown.

There are three registrations under Bull Mastiffs in 1912. They are Diamond, d, Mr C. Richardson, sired by Mr Bishop's Thorney Wood Terror out of Mr Matthew's Clifton Lass, May 14th 1911. Grip, d, Mr C. Richardson, sired by Mr Bishop's Thorney Wood Terror out of Mr Matthew's Clifton Lass, July 10th 1907. Osmaston Daisy, b, Mr C. Richardson, sired by Mr

Bishop's Thorney Wood Terror out of Mr Biggs' Osmaston Topsy, June 1908. I cannot accept these pedigrees as accurate. Why? Thorney Wood has been split into two words; I cannot find any transfer for the ownership of the original Thorneywood Terror from Mr Burton to Mr Bishop; and the original Clifton Lass was whelped March 25th 1894.

REGISTRATIONS OF CROSSBREEDS

Retracing my research it was interesting to note that as far back as June 1905 the Kennel Club were beginning to have problems with cross-breeds. They issued the following statement: "The Kennel Club Committee have arrived at an important decision regarding the registration of cross-breed dogs. In future, in the event of any of the parents or ancestors nominated on the registration form of a dog being of a different breed from the dog itself these facts must be clearly stated on the Registration Form."

In November of the same year the following was published: "At a meeting of the General Committee on November 14th, the following recommendations of the Sub-Committee on Crossbreeds were received and adopted: "That Crossbreeds of the first generation be allowed registration and entry in the Kennel Club Stud Book provided:-

1. That they be entered under the heading of "Crossbreeds" and the names of the breeds or varieties making the cross be distinctly stated.
2. That the cross be made between two varieties of a breed or be such a cross as meets the Kennel Club approval.
3. That the Kennel Club may refuse registration and entry in the Kennel Club Stud Book if they think fit.
4. That the progeny resulting from cross-bred dogs mated back to the same breed as either of the parent factors (second generation) shall be registered under similar conditions.
5. The progeny resulting from the second cross (second generation) bred back to the same original breed, as before used to produce second generation, shall be allowed to be registered and entered in the Kennel Club Stud Book under the heading of the original pure breed from which and where with the out cross has been made."

Whether this meant that a cross-bred Bull-Mastiff could eventually have progeny registered as Bulldogs or Mastiffs, I do not know. What do you think?

Although the General Committee's recommendation stated that the names of the breeds or varieties making the cross should be distinctly stated, this rarely happened in the case of Bullmastiffs. From 1901 to 1920 twenty-two came under Crossbreeds and were merely headed Bull Mastiffs. In most cases neither the sire nor the dam were registered. Two were registered as Bull and Mastiff, and one as Mastiff and Bull Mastiff. The latter is of great interest – Lion, d, Mr G. H. Jeffworth, sired by Mr J. Barrowcliffe's Pedro (Mastiff) out of his Gyp (Bull Mastiff), June 18th 1914. J. Barrowcliffe bred both Mastiffs and Bull Mastiffs and he was one of the first judges to award Challenge Certificates to Bull Mastiffs. He judged the breed at Manchester Championship Show in 1929 and he awarded the third and qualifying CC to Vic Smith's Tiger Prince. Barrowcliffe's original kennel name was Stapleford or Stableford and this was used on many unregistered dogs and bitches. In later years he registered the affix Parkvale. Tiger Prince's dam was Princess Poppy and her sire was Stapleford Brutus (UNR). In 1925 Stapleford Brutus was registered under Crossbreeds (Bull Mastiff) as Brutus of Parkvale, d, Mr J. Barrowcliffe; sired by Bulwell Muggs (UNR) out of Bess (UNR); breeder/owner; January 15th 1917. Among the Bulldog registrations in October 1905 there was African Lion (Bulldog-Mastiff), d, Mr W. H. Cook, sired by the Hon. A. H. Strutt's Kingston Tiger out of Mr H. Dyer's Gotham Furry, August

Ch. Young Mary Bull, born 1914.

Photo: Thomas Fall.

20th 1904. Was Gotham Furry bred by Mr Dye or Dyer, whose Mastiff Gotham Lion won first prize at the Gamekeepers' Annual Show in 1903?

In April 1921 under Crossbreeds (Bull Mastiff) there was a single registration "For Competition" – Sir Roger, d, Mr G. Hammett, sired by Poor Joe (Bull Mastiff) out of Peggy (Bull Mastiff UNR); breeder Mr Jerrard; July 17th 1920. In August 1921 under Mastiffs "For Competition" there was Poor Jerry, d, H. Page; Poor Joe, d, Peggy (UNR); breeder Mr Gerrard; July 17th 1920. Was it a coincidence that the names of both sires and dams were the same and also the dates of birth? The name of the breeder differed in the initial letter only. In April 1920 under Mastiffs there was Poor Joe, d, Mr R. J. Burch, sired by Brompton Duke out of Galazora, June 17th 1916. In June 1922 two Mastiffs were registered "Not For Competition". The second was Peggy, b, Mr A. Gerard; pedigree and breeder unknown, August 29th 1918.

The registration system must have been very lax because in January 1922, one Mastiff was registered "For Competition": Diana of Dermot, b, Mr A. Baggaley, sire King Baldur, dam Penkhull Lady; breeder Mrs F. Harvey; July 26th 1921. In April 1922 one Crossbreed was registered: Binkie, b, Mr and Mrs H. F. Elliott, sire King Baldur (Mastiff) dam Penkhull Lady (Crossbreed); breeder Mr F. Harvey – was it Mr or Mrs? August 1922 under Mastiffs we find: Clayton Betty, b; Clayton Peggy, b; Jersey Lion, d; and Shirebrook Lady, b. The sire of all four was King Baldur and the dam Penkhill Lady. Just to add to the confusion, Mr F. Harvey bred the first three and Mr Harvey-Fenton the last one. Even the dates of birth varied from July 25th 1922 (obviously a mistake) to July 25th and 26th 1921. Even the dam's name had changed to Penkhill. All four were later corrected and said to be "Crossbreeds". The same sire and dam appeared later in both Mastiff and Bull Mastiff registrations.

King Baldur, who later became a champion, was registered in April 1918. King Baldur, d, Miss M. D. Hitchings, by Mr R. J. Burch's Young John Bull out of his Young Mary Bull; June 8th 1917. Young John Bull and Young Mary Bull (who became a Champion) were litter brother and sister. They were registered in July 1915, Mrs D. Berry, sired by owner's Brompton Duke out of her Galazora, October 5th 1914. They were full brother and sister to Poor Joe. Some old pedigrees have changed the name of the dam once again to Parkhull Lady, who was registered in July 1920 as a Crossbreed "For Competition: Mr H. Besley, sired by Mr J. Barrowcliffe's Stapleford Agrippa

Vindictive: The subject of controversial registration.

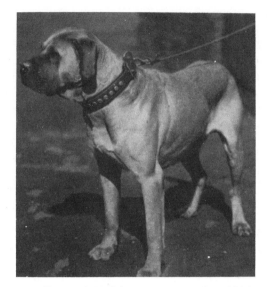

Farcroft Fidelity: Registered in 1922, and went on to have a significant influence on the breed.

(Bull Mastiff UNR) out of his Helen (Bull Mastiff UNR) February 29th 1920. In July 1922 another well-publicised dog was registered – Farcroft Fidelity, d, (Bull Mastiff), Mr S. E. Moseley; sire Vindictive (UNR), dam Farcroft Faithful (UNR); breeder, owner; September 4th 1921. In the re-registrations for July 1925 there was one Bull Mastiff, Farcroft Fidelity. There was one change – the sire was Shireland Vindictive, also unregistered. As so much has been said and written about this dog in the past, it may be as well to lay his ghost now. Among odd pieces of paper which I have collected there is part of an article by Mr E. D. Iliff who used to write for one of the dog periodicals. It runs as follows: "With regard to Mr Barnard's statement that Farcroft Fidelity was the grandson (not the great-grandson) of Wellington Marquis, I have enquired of Mr S. E. Moseley, who bred Fidelity. Here is his reply: 'I sent Farcroft Faithful (Fidelity's dam) to Osmaston Viper for stud service. Viper was then in the hands of Mr Pierce, MRCVS of Shireland Road, London. He wrote that Viper was getting old and could not serve Faithful, and that he had put her to his other dog. In our correspondence Mr Pierce had only mentioned and submitted pedigrees of Viper and Vindictive. I very naturally thought that his other dog was Vindictive. Puppies were born on September 4th 1921; I registered Farcroft Fidelity, one of the litter, as by Vindictive. In later correspondence I found Vindictive was not the sire of Fidelity, who was sired by Vindictive's son, Shireland Vindictive. I immediately put the matter and correspondence before the Kennel Club, and they on June 5th 1925, re-registered him as by Shireland Vindictive. The certificate number is A531. The particulars of re-registration appeared in the Kennel Club Gazette 544, of July 1925. Some pedigrees were, of course, issued according to the original registration, but very wide publicity was given to correct the error when it was discovered'. Let us hope that this matter, which is only of academic interest to most of us, since Fidelity's influence on the breed is well established, may now be allowed to drop."

Some of the books which have been written about the breed state that Farcroft Fidelity was the first Bullmastiff entered in the Kennel Club Stud Book. He was not. This may have come from the fact that he was the first Bullmastiff to win a first prize at Crufts before CCs were offered to the breed. In 1928, when CCs were first on offer, there were four championship shows and Fidelity was placed first in the last one. Four dogs and seven bitches were given stud book numbers – the first being Tiger Prince 60 JJ. Details of breeder; owner; date of birth; sire; dam and also colour were given with each entry. The paternal grand-sire of Tiger Prince was given as Farcroft Fidelity 1960 JJ; but Farcroft Fidelity was not entered in the Kennel Club Stud Book; nor has he been entered up to the present date.

Before leaving Farcroft Fidelity I am reminded of a pedigree sent to me by the late Charles F. Binney, one-time Secretary of the Kennel Club. I was tracing the ancestry of our line and I came across a dog which I knew had been owned by Charles Binney, Thorgils of Threadholt. I found its sire, Ch. Simba and its dam, Beauty of Billéden but I couldn't find the dog, so I wrote to Charles Binney for help. He was very kind and sent me a copy of the pedigree of the dog who was originally registered as Jumbo of Billéden. He was bred by a Mrs Parfrement in 1933. The paternal grandsire of both Ch. Simba and Beauty of Billéden was given as Farcroft Fidelity, whose sire was Shireland Vindictive. The sire of Shireland Vindictive was given as Wellington Marquis. There was no mention of Vindictive. Shireland Vindictive was entered as by Wellington Marquis ex Nuneaton Nance. By the side of the last two names there was a cross and between them the word Mastiff, thus indicating a Mastiff Crossbreed. Marquis was a Bulldog by Hail Stone ex Comedy Queen (UNR). An advertisement in *Our Dogs* Christmas Supplement, December 14th 1917 stated that Wellington Marquis was dark brindle and weighed 54 lbs. In the same supplement there was an advertisement for a dog whom we could assume to be his son 'Vindictive 90 lb brindle Bull Mastiff at stud – one of the gamest and most active living. Fee 2 guineas. Peirce's Animal Hospital'.

In 1919 Peirce advertises in the Christmas Supplement again: "Savage young Bull Mastiff bitch wanted immediately; must be real Bull Mastiff without spot of Dane in her; Thorneywood Terror or Osmaston strain; dark brindle preferred but dark fawn not objected to if brindle bred; black mask indispensable; not less than 75 lb weight and must stand the test. Write with full particulars to Peirce's Animal Hospital, 62 Shirland Road, Paddington". Also in the wanted column was another interesting advertisement. "Wanted: Bull Mastiff or Bloodhound or Bull Mastiff–Bloodhound cross; Moseley, Farcroft, Burslem." Mr Moseley also bred German Shepherd Dogs.

Ch. Simba, owned by the Marquess of Londonderry.

Could this be where the large ears and the occasional long coats came in? Arthur Craven FZS wrote the first book on the breed, *The Bull-Mastiff As I Know It,* in the 1930s and he must have seen some strange animals masquerading as Bullmastiffs. I cannot do better than to quote his words: "Few breeds have suffered the same indignity as the Bull-Mastiff; as in the past, on account of them not being fully established, a few unscrupulous so-called fanciers, to suit ends best known to themselves, at one time attempted to improve them (as they thought), and resorted to crossing with their animals the Great Dane, St Bernard, Newfoundland, and possibly the Bloodhound to a slight degree. This resulted in a temporary setback for the breed, and had it not been for the loyalty of those fanciers who were determined that no foreign blood should be mixed with that of the Bull-Mastiff, the breed today would not have been in its present position.

"The Bull-Mastiff if properly bred should carry its own trade mark. To any person it should be easily recognizable, as neither Mastiff nor Bulldog. If you see a so-called Bull-Mastiff with a shaggy coat, look upon its breeding as being alien; possibly some blood of the St Bernard, or even the Newfoundland, is running through its veins. If you likewise see a Bull-Mastiff with a Great Dane muzzle, pass it by; you cannot afford to take risks, and no animal that is termed a Bull-Mastiff (pure-bred) should resemble any breed other than the two which are claimed to have been originally used. In the past so-called Bull-Mastiffs have been bred that had a coat of such length as to make us realize the danger which the breed was at one period running; still, we should remember that when we see an animal with a coat of a length that calls for stripping, it is not a genuine Bull-Mastiff. A true-bred specimen may occasionally vary to a slight degree in length of coat, but we should remember we have only one variety which is termed "smooth coat", and if you drop across a "rough coat", irrespective of how good its other points appear to be, I would advise you to look with suspicion upon it, and under no circumstances whatever either purchase or breed from it." If only Arthur Craven was alive today! Even so, his advice is as sound today as it was sixty years ago.

Many of the pedigrees and registrations carry unregistered dogs and bitches which make it very difficult to prove the true breeding of any line. S. E. Moseley laid down a blue print which looks good on paper. "The Bull-Mastiff should be fawn or brindle in colour (the former is perhaps the most favoured at the moment), while a little white is permissible, showing his inheritance of Bulldog blood. His weight should be 90 lb to 110 lbs, his height 27 to 28 inches (a bitch may be 10 lbs less in weight and an inch less in height than a dog). I would rather a 25 or 26 inches and quality than these 30 inches and over dogs of Great Dane type. A Bull-Mastiff should be active and free from cowhock or splay feet, a perfectly assimilated 60 per cent Mastiff and 40 per cent Bulldog. Little, if any, care has been taken in breeding some so called Bull-Mastiffs. To produce a dog I had in mind, I set out with a well defined plan. Having planned my work I worked my plan for my first pillar on the following foundation. Taking a Mastiff bitch and a Bulldog, I produce a 50-50. A bitch of these I mate to a Mastiff dog and this gave me 75 per cent Mastiff and 25 per cent Bull bitch, which I mate to a 50-50 dog. A bitch from this litter, 62.5 per cent Mastiff 37.5 per cent Bull I mate to a 50-50 dog and a bitch from this litter I put to a 62.5 per cent Mastiff 37.5 per cent Bulldog, which gave me approximately my ideal – 60 per cent Mastiff and 40 per cent Bull, I repeat this from other blood lines as an outcross and thus I established my "Farcroft" strain, and the Bull-Mastiff, a standard breed of set type, which breed true – like produces like. This is fixing a type, not merely breeding a crossbreed."

How I wish I could accept Mr Moseley's plan. Even the white has been found on Mastiffs as well as Bulldogs. Ch. Wolsey (1873) had four white feet and a white flash under his chest. In Clifford Hubbard's *The Bullmastiff Handbook* there is a copy of one of Thomas Bewick's wood engravings of a British Mastiff of about 1730 and this dog carries an excessive amount of white on his head, neck and body. Over the past fifty years I have attempted to build up five generation pedigrees for every champion awarded its title under Kennel Club rules. The first is Ch. Farcroft Silvo: a brindle bitch bred by Mr Moseley; sire, Hamil Grip; dam, Farcroft Belltong; DOB March 18th 1925. At the time of her registration both parents were unregistered. This was amended in August 1927: Hamil Grip, d, Mr S. E. Moseley; sire Hamil Terror (UNR); dam Hamil Lady (UNR); breeder, owner; November 1920. Farcroft Belltong, b, Mr S. E. Moseley; sire Farcroft Valient (UNR); dam Farcroft Galant (UNR); breeder, owner; February 1921. Cross checks with the Kennel Club Stud Books show that Moseley had many unregistered bitches which came up on a number of pedigrees. Three or four sires were used and, although they were registered, it was difficult to prove their ancestry. Many wellknown Mastiff names came up, but it was impossible to prove continuity of breeding. The one dog which carries any authentic lineage is Baldur's Best, d, Mrs E. Bowers; sire King Baldur, dam, Penkhull Lady; Mr F. Harvey; February 20th 1922. As we know King Baldur was a pure-bred Mastiff and it is reasonable to assume that Penkhull Lady carried a fair share of Mastiff blood.

In October 1924 the General Committee of the Kennel Club considered a recommendation that if a new breed should register 80 dogs in four years, ending the preceding December 31st, it should be added to the Register for the coming year, and that a breed should not be entitled to Challenge Certificates if, in any year ending December 31st previous, there were fewer than 20 registrations in the breed. In the *Kennel Gazette* for December 1924 came the following statement: "In our October issue it was announced that a breed shall be automatically added to the Register of Breeds, thus becoming entitled to the allocation of Challenge Certificates, in the year following its accession to the Register when 80 of that breed shall have been registered during a maximum period of four years and providing that at least three years have elapsed since the first registration in that breed. With reference to Bull-Mastiffs, the Committee at their meeting of the 2nd inst., decided that it is prepared to open a section among the 'Any Other Variety' registrations for Bull-Mastiffs if pure-bred as such, and when sufficient be registered under this heading as such, according to the scale mentioned above, the breed would be eligible for a place on the Register of Breeds. It is of course, most important to observe the distinction between a Bull-Mastiff (Pure-bred) and a Bull-Mastiff (Cross-bred); the former being a dog bred with both parents and the preceding three generations all Bull-Mastiffs without the introduction of a Mastiff or a Bulldog. The term Bull-Mastiff (Cross-bred) implies the existence of a definite cross which has not yet been bred out according to Regulation 12 of the Regulations of Registration."

From 1925 under the heading of 'Any Other Breed or Variety of British, Colonial, or Foreign Dogs Not Classified' there are Bull-Mastiffs and Bull-Mastiffs (Crossbreeds). Amongst the Bull-Mastiffs there are many with unregistered sires or dams. How the ancestry of these could be proven is beyond me. Some of the Bull-Mastiffs (Crossbreeds) were carrying identical blood lines. October 1927 saw 16 registrations in the Register of Breeds, headed 'Bull-Mastiffs (Pure Bred)'. Of these 16 registrations, one was later cancelled, Farcroft Felon's Frayeur became a champion, and one, Bridewell Night Patrol, was one of the first seven bitches entered in the Kennel Club Stud Book in 1929. From then on, only four were registered as Crossbreeds, but in March, April, May, June, July, August, September and October 1938 various registrations were made as 'Parent Registrations'. There were fourteen altogether; seven of them being registered by Mrs S. E. Moseley. Six of these had sire: Henchman of the Hamil (gs Harmony of the Hamil, gd Hereditary of the Hamil); dam: Habitue of the Hamil (gs Haughty of the Hamil, gd Heedful of the Hamil). I cannot recall seeing any of these names on a pedigree; most certainly not the pedigree of a champion.

Moseley certainly believed in the old adage that it pays to advertise. He issued a number of

Ch. Springwell Major: Exported to South Africa.

small booklets advertising his stud dogs. These booklets had photographs and pedigrees and were issued in the late 1920s. In the first one there is a review taken from *Town and Country News,* July 25th 1925. It was written by the editor, E. Marchant Smith. "The latest dog to be registered by the Kennel club as a pure-bred is the Bull-Mastiff, although he has long been appealed for as the true all-British dog. At Farcroft Kennels, Burslem, the Bull-Mastiff is the favourite of the owner, Mr S. E. Moseley, who also keeps and trains Alsatian Wolfdogs and Bloodhound-Mastiffs. There are fifteen Bull-Mastiff brood bitches and three stud dogs at Farcroft, and over a hundred puppies bred yearly are not sufficient to meet the demand.

"Mr Moseley's opinion, that Bull-Mastiffs are the coming dog, finds many supporters in this country. Now they are on the show bench they are sure to beat many breeds in popular favour. As police dogs Bull-Mastiffs are without equal; their qualities are more genuine than showy. Easily trained, their good noses make them excellent trackers. They are faithful and fearless but not ferocious; a staunch game guard; an affectionate and intelligent companion. Mr S. E. Moseley is the oldest breeder-trainer and has the largest kennels of Bullmastiffs in this country. During last year he exported dogs to Africa, America, Canada, France, Holland, Belgium, Egypt and Federated Malay States. In the last, the Bull-Mastiffs were to be used for boar hunting. All brood bitches are kept at walk in the country. Consequently, puppies are raised under ideal conditions. When Bull-Mastiffs become in due course eligible for Championship Certificates, it is safe to say that one of the first names to figure prominently on the coveted cards will be the title 'Farcroft'."

Looking back on this review, there is more than a hint of poetic licence. If Moseley was breeding a hundred puppies a year, the majority of them were unregistered or registered without his kennel name. In 1925 there were 68 registrations; 46 by different breeders and 22 by Moseley. Of the latter, only seven carried the Farcroft affix and one of these was later cancelled. However, Farcroft Silvo was one of the seven and she did become the breed's first champion. As for the exports, the first dog officially exported with an export licence issued by the Kennel Club was Farcroft Export in July 1930, followed by Farcroft Fidget in August. Both went to United States. There were no further exports carrying the Farcroft affix.

Until January 1945 all the exports with an export licence issued by the Kennel Club went to the US. That month showed Sapper of Le Tasyll being exported to Canada. One of the outstanding exports was Jeanette of Brooklands bred by Mr T. Pennington and exported to John W. Cross Jnr.

in America in January 1936. She became the first Bullmastiff Champion in the US. When John Cross's health deteriorated, Jeanette came back to this country and she continued her winning ways, becoming the 37th British champion.

A famous dog who went out to guard the diamond mines in South Africa was Ch. Springwell Major. He was bred by W. & G. R. Richardson and transferred to Dorothy Nash in May 1939. He was transferred to De Beers Consolidated Mines Ltd in December 1939. Thanks to my friend Graham Hicks we were able to track him down in South Africa, even though he was exported without an export licence. A letter from the secretary of the Kennel Union of Southern Africa written to Graham Hicks, dated April 16th 1986 stated: "On the upper portion of the page, registrations are recorded as February 6th 1940 whilst on top of the following page as February 15th 1940. There was, and still is, no compunction (sic) on anyone importing a dog to register it with the Kennel Union unless they intend to breed from it or exhibit it at a Kennel Union recognized show. Thus it would be very hard to determine the actual date of import.

"In the 1930s various organizations such as De Beers were importing dogs, which in many cases were initially registered with the Kennel Union, under the kennel name 'De Beers' etc. Since then many organizations have built up their own internal breeding programmes with pedigreed dogs which are in many cases not registered with us, the main reason being that they are bred as guard dogs." The upper portion of the page referred to begins with No 48761 and concerns a Sealyham dog. Two thirds of the way down the page comes: 48786, Ch. Adamant Springwell Major, D, Bull-Mastiff, De Beers Cons. Ltd. Ch. Roger of the Fenns – Lady Dinah of Springwell, 20 October 1935, Messrs W. P. G. K. Richardson. Since Farcroft Export went out to the US, Bullmastiffs have been exported to the far corners of the world. It would take too long to list all the countries concerned, but the last four were Chile, Slovenia, Ukraine and Lithuania.

Ch. Jubilee Captain Fantastic CD: The Bullmastiff is known for its courage – and for its docility.
Photo: Peter Aczel.

Chapter Two

THE BULLMASTIFF CHARACTER

If we look at the Breed Standard, the section devoted to characteristics has changed very little over the years since the breed was first recognised. Before the Breed Standard was laid down, the National Bull-Mastiff Police Dog Club produced a rough guide drawn up by S. E. Moseley and accepted by the Club. The opening sentence read: "In general appearance the Bull-Mastiff is a noble symmetrical animal with well knit frame, powerful but active, courageous but docile." At that time points were awarded up to a total of 100 and the first items listed were '"Symmetry and general character – 10". When the standard was officially drawn up general appearance and characteristics came under separate headings and the one for characteristics is still the same: "Characteristics. The temperament of the Bullmastiff combines high spirits, reliability, activity, endurance and alertness."

A PLEA FOR AN UNRECOGNISED BREED OF BRITISH DOG
This is part of an article written by Count Vivian Hollender for the March 1911 issue of *The Kennel*. Count Hollender owned a Bull-Mastiff, Nada The Fearless, and he was the fourth judge to award CCs in the breed. "I now wish to make a plea for a mongrel, or rather a cross-bred dog, and urge his claims. Perhaps it is hardly fair to designate the Bull-Mastiff by the word mongrel, as at the term mongrel, or cross-bred, now-a-days aristocratic dog lovers shiver. The public knows very little of the qualities of the Bull-Mastiff, and what is more, that it has been in existence for some considerable time; and if it is useless to make an appeal for this dog from a sentimental point of view, I do so quite conscientiously, knowing that this dog is the bravest, the most perfect guard and protector in the world. I owe, however, my introduction to the breed to Mr J. H. Bennett, of 99 Broomspring Lane, Sheffield.

"Before recounting any reminiscences or tales of this breed I have just set forth a few plain facts reproduced from papers. I am condensing the plain unvarnished truth, and not giving the whole of the extracts which were published. Some people may run away with the idea that these dogs are savages, but they are trained to obey a command, and, curious as it may be to relate, in every instance the dogs who have captured poachers, thieves and desperadoes, have always been muzzled. No Airedale could chase and down men armed with sticks or gun barrels and hold them down until assistance arrived. Bull-Mastiffs know no fear and are never beaten. Naturally all this requires a course of training, which is dealt with in *The Training of Dogs as Guards and Defenders* – at least I think this is the title of the book. The dog is started at about ten months old on a dummy and is gradually taught to face a man with anything in his hand. Were the police armed with these dogs in dangerous districts there would be very few murders. Criminals will face anything rather than a savage dog, and if they are frightened at Airedales, they would be

Ch. Jubilee Governor. A powerfully-built dog, the Bullmastiff was bred as a guard dog, and in olden times used to help gamekeepers apprehend poachers.

Photo: Peter Aczel.

A life of luxury is high on the Bullmastiff's list of priorities.

Photo courtesy: Pentax, UK.

absolutely panic-stricken if they had to face a Bull-Mastiff, which is not pretty at the best of times. Moreover, it is very difficult to fire at a dog and hit it, although some of these poor dogs have lost their lives in saving people. They are highly intelligent and seem to be possessed of wonderful quickness and scenting power, and for a long time I confess I was baffled to find out whence they got their speed and wonderful noses, as neither the Bull-dog nor the Mastiff could be looked on as very fast dogs or possessing wonderful scent. Personally I think at times the strain of Bloodhound has been introduced, and that the old fashioned Bull-dog was used and not the modern dog.

"I think it says something for the sagacity of these dogs that when Mr Bennett was a little boy out with his sister, they were frightened by a tramp 'Watch him, Dick,' said Mr Bennett to the dog. The dog in his hurry to get at the tramp, knocked over Mr Bennett's little sister into a shallow running stream; he came back and pulled her out first, and then held up the tramp until the children got back to their house, and was holding him up when Mr Bennett senior arrived. On another occasion, when their father and mother were out, a man tried to force an entrance into the front door, saying he would wait for their parents' return. They had been playing in the hall with a rocking-horse, and the man had to push somewhat to get in at the front door. Meanwhile, the servant let loose one of the Bull-Mastiffs. The dog held the man up in the hall from 9 o'clock that night until 3 o'clock the next morning when the parents came back from the party which they had attended. The children sat up in blankets too frightened to go to bed; no one could call the dog off; food, everything was tried and the man promised and cried to be allowed to go. The front door was still open and the cold and snow were blowing in. No one dare shut the door and all the children's coaxing could not move the dog. When Mr Bennett senior arrived, one half of the man was numbed through cold and still the dog stood it all, holding up the intruder. The police were sent for, and the man in question was found to be a notorious house-breaker and scoundrel and was relieved of his jemmy and revolver. As Mr Bennett tersely puts it – revolvers are not much use if a dog won't let you draw them. Mr Biggs, who is an old man, was set upon by poachers one night and desperately attacked. It was a melee, and a struggle for life on the ground, and his bitch, though terribly knocked about, 'ousted' the three poachers in the end, and during the whole of the struggle she stepped over and about her master's body like a lamb. I have many other instances to relate about these dogs and their masters, and proofs shown as puppies of the extraordinary character they develop in their affections. This I shall do at a later period, and I hope in the meanwhile I shall have interested many who will look at the claims of a dog that is not only all British but combines wonderful pluck and endurance with the gentleness of a lamb, and whose only aim and request is, if necessary, to take its death serving its master or mistress. One cannot buy devotion; the next best thing is to buy a Bull-Mastiff.

"It is only right to chronicle that, curiously enough, the biggest authorities on the Bull-Mastiff (Mr S. E. Moseley and Mr W. Burton) disagree about the exact origin of the breed. I am inclined to think that the Bloodhound has occasionally played its part and, in a few instances, the Great Dane. Mr Burton considers the Bull-Mastiff rather dangerous to go about in the ordinary way, but then he is speaking of the trained dog. My contention, and that of the majority of authorities, is that the dog has all the pluck, power and endurance to take punishment that is necessary, and this can be developed or not according to in whose hands the dog may be. A savage dog does not mean a plucky dog, and any savage animal not under control should be shot, irrespective of the breed. Naturally the Bull-Mastiff might have a tendency to be more savage, and certainly more determined in its attack. The majority of breeders from my own personal experience tell me that they are one of the safest dogs in the world to be trusted with children or ladies. It is true they might be more alert than most watch-dogs and a little keener to tackle anybody while they are guarding, but that is the beauty of the breed."

THE EARLY YEARS OF REGISTRATION

In his first advertising booklet for the Farcroft Kennels, S. E. Moseley stressed that the Bull-Mastiff stood above all other dogs as a staunch and faithful companion. He quoted the example of the dam of Farcroft Fidelity who died whilst defending her master on the Yorkshire moors. The owner wrote to Moseley the following week asking for a puppy of the same strain. In his letter he stated: "The children wanted her brought home, so I carried her for two miles over the moors and buried her where we can see the grave of the best pal man or child ever had. True until death!" In the same booklet, Mr Morris of Stafford, who owned Stand Aside, a brindle son of Farcroft Fidelity, said of his dog: "He is greatly admired – at a distance. His looks belie him, for he is really the most even-tempered dog I have ever seen. He plays with my little boy of three-and-a-half years old, and never even bumps into him. The boy takes bones out of his mouth, but he does not resent it in any way; a firm guard but in no way ferocious. My association with the Bull-Mastiff dates back to the time when practically every game-preserving estate in Great Britain owned these dogs, and their merits were often discussed with greater pride by the Gamekeeper than the merits of the Gundogs, for his life often depended on the staunchness of his Bull-Mastiff."

BRITISH WAR DOGS

The following was taken from a book written by Lieutenant Colonel E. H. Richardson who trained dogs for the British Army, the Police Force and similar bodies. "I remember the case of a very large fine Bull-Mastiff, which was offered to the War Dog School. It had never been off the chain for four years, as it was so savage that no one could approach it with safety. With great difficulty it was sent to the school, and had to be taken out of the railway van by means of long poles. On arrival it was fastened to a kennel, but its behaviour was so outrageous, and as there seemed to be a risk of its breaking away and attacking the staff, the opinion was formed that it would have to be destroyed. Preparations were made to this end, when Mrs Richardson pleaded to have one more day for a final experiment. For two hours she stood near the dog, speaking to it softly. Gradually she edged nearer still, speaking, but never looking at the animal. She discerned that underneath the creature's savage behaviour, there was a highly strung, sensitive nature, and that if confidence could be established, the ferocity, which was merely due to soreness of mind and fear, would vanish.

"After a time, she was able to lean against the kennel, and then very gently her hand was laid on the large brown head, and permission was given for her to stroke the satin ears. With very quiet movement, she unfastened the chain and slipped on a lead and led the poor beast away. Its gratitude and delight at being treated as an ordinary trustworthy dog was unbounded, and when I was making a round of inspection later that day, I found the great beast seated at her feet, looking up with adoring eyes at his saviour. After this the dog was the great favourite with all the staff, and absolutely reliable, while still retaining all its guarding qualifications as regards strangers and it did some very useful work for its country."

BULLMASTIFFS IN SOUTH WEST AFRICA

This article was published over twenty years ago in *The American Bullmastiff* and was by courtesy of the *South African Bullmastiff News*. Alas! the name of the writer was not given. "The first Bull-Mastiff, imported from England, arrived in Windhoek, South West Africa, in early 1928. This was a bitch, Farcroft Vigil, fawn with a black mask, aged about four years, said to be in whelp, but was not. She was a very good-tempered animal, and kindly to small children, and without being at all disagreeable or dangerous – an excellent guard – not only because of her forbidding appearance but her technique was perfect. Our house in Klein Windhoek, stood on a hill, the large grounds stretching downwards to the front gate which was some distance away. Near the house were twenty-five large steps leading up to the front step. Vigil lived up to her name, and she knew when someone was entering the gate, would meet him silently and 'shoulder' him each time he made a movement towards the step. No one ever got up the steps without calling me, and the moment I arrived and spoke to Vigil, she allowed the visitor to progress. Occasionally, a misbehaving child was given a smack. In a trice Vigil was there and held my arm gently in her great jaws; even I must not hit children. Remember, she was not brought up with our young family, she arrived as an adult, and straight from kennelling. One day, I had her walking beside me in the main street. As we passed a cafe, a small boy in the doorway dashed inside yelling, 'Boetie, hier is n leeu!' (little brother, come, here is a lion), creating great excitement and alarm.

"Farcroft Joe was our next import, as Vigil had been given a great deal of publicity and interest. She was exhibited once in Cape Town under 'Foreign Breeds' (there being no Bull-Mastiff Section in those days) and many people asked me for puppies for guards. So came Joe, a very dark brindle. He was somewhat smaller type than Vigil and extremely active. The type of Bull-Mastiff in those days varied considerably. His temperament was also good, he honoured the 'shouldering' perfected by Vigil, but he also barked to let me know, and as a consequence terrified any native who unsuspectingly got through the gate before noticing the sentries. The shrieking could then be heard far and wide, and the barking and 'shouldering' more active. But never did either bite the intruder, who naturally *never* again entered the gate, and quite soon all natives were warned and I was known by an unspellable name which meant – The mistress with the dogs with the big mouths."

Reading this, I am intrigued with the word 'shouldering', especially as no explanation is given. In by-gone days when the Bullmastiff was used to detain poachers, the dog would spring forward, hitting the man on the shoulders with his front paws. This would catch the man off balance and he would fall backwards, flat on his back. The dog would stand over the man, front legs and feet on his shoulders, daring the man to move. Not a pleasant prospect, thinking of the jaws on a Bullmastiff head! Nowadays, I think this trait has been toned down, and many Bullmastiffs spring forward, placing their front paws on a visitor's shoulders. It is not a powerful movement and there is no aggression but it does tend to upset people who do not know the Bullmastiff.

THE BRITISH BULLMASTIFF LEAGUE'S HANDBOOK

I am indebted to the British Bullmastiff League for three of the items in their handbook published in October 1948. The first is headed 'Judy, my companion' – a delightful pen picture by Rafael Sabatini, the famous novelist. "Dignity is her second name. She never whimpers, scratches or fusses for what she wants, or is ever importunate in any of the ways canine and human. It is only her velvety eyes that plead for admittance as she gazes at me through the French windows of my study. After a little while if I do not open to admit her she will move away, as calmly resigned as if she understood that some good reason exists why her admittance is not convenient. More commonly, however, the glass door is opened. Even then she waits, looking at me until I say 'Come in'. And once in, as I return to my writing-table, a quietly uttered, 'Lie down, Judy,' stretches this very understanding dog behind my chair. There she will lie peacefully, hour after hour perhaps, until she sees me rise.

"As powerful as she is imperturbable, she is as gentle as she is powerful. The tenderness with which she can wield her massive jaws is an abiding mystery. As she walks with me by the river a fleeing rabbit will set her in pursuit, but without bloodthirst. It is not often that she will overtake the fleet little coney before it has gained the sanctuary of its bolt-hole. But it has happened that her great jaws have snapped audibly, and but little of the rabbit has remained protruding from them. I have imagined the little beast mangled out of recognition, reduced to squelch of blood and fur. Yet, after a moment, Judy will drop it and the rabbit will scamper off, unhurt, to be caught again, until I call Judy off so as to put an end to a cruelty entirely unconscious on her part. Her only aim has been to play with the little creature. To the word of command she will subdue at once even her natural impulses.

"To the water by which we live she has taken as if she were a spaniel, and to cross to me if I am on the other bank, and unless I order her to remain where she is, she will breast the wide river anywhere, and easily, no matter how strong and how swift the current. As a watch-dog her intelligence evokes wonder. Friendly to all by day, and hostile to none who enters the grounds, yet after dark, at the least unusual movement, or the fall of a strange foot, she at once departs from her normally silent habit and her deep-toned voice gives warning. A more ideal companion never lived; affectionate, obedient, loyal and self-contained, she is yet joyous and playful whenever encouraged to it. Observing actions that reflect the working of an intelligence that up to a point is swift and sure, you may wonder, as I do, why it should stop abruptly when that point is reached, why, indeed, any limit should be set to its compass. This may lead you to reflect that perhaps for man, as for the dog, there is a barrier, which some do not even suspect, beyond which the mind is impotent to function. Meanwhile let us be thankful that canine intelligence ceases where it does. If they went further, the dog might think less of his owner."

The second item is headed 'In Praise of the Bullmastiff' and it was written by the Patron of the League, Captain Gerald Lowry, OStJ, the first officer blinded in the Great War.

February 24th 1937

My Dear Captain Towler,
My very best wishes for the success of the Bullmastiff.
Little did I think when you so generously sent me Biddy, the Bullmastiff bitch, what the puppy would come to be in my life, and how often have both my wife and I blessed you since for your kindness.
And then, later, when we acquired the brindle, Mike, we felt and still feel that we have got a family of absorbing interest.
Biddy is simply human the way in which she speaks to you and understands everything you say. They are both so beautifully clean and strong that it does one good to see them, and they are so wonderfully gentle. Biddy makes a splendid watch-dog.
I often wonder how I got through those years of blindness from 1914 without my beloved friends Biddy and Mike.

Believe me
Yours very sincerely
(Signed) G Lowry

21 Upper Berkeley Street
Great Cumberland Place
W1.

How better to finish the early years than with a poem which was included at the end of the handbook:

Breathes there the man with soul so dead,
Who never to himself hath said,
"Look at that fine, that noble head!"
BULLMASTIFF!

Need you a guard, an honest friend,
One who will serve you to the end,
With loyalty that nought can bend?
BULLMASTIFF!

Mark how that great, that noble hound,
Whose brow is knit in thoughts profound,
Is always in his habits, sound
BULLMASTIFF!

A friend to you, he knows no fear,
An honest fellow, conscience clear,
A dog that you will hold most dear,
BULLMASTIFF!

Alas! The writer may just as well have signed himself or herself 'anonymous', as the only identification lies in two letters, I. M. However, these three items give perfect pen-portraits of the character of the Bullmastiff as it was fifty years ago.

KELLY

Our first bitch, Kelly, was a great favourite with most people, especially children. The school children all knew her by name and when she whelped her first litter (during the school holidays) one child appeared with his mother, asking permission to see the puppies. They were three weeks old. My husband was manager of a hostel and access for traffic was over a wide cattle grid. There was at that time wide areas of common land, and sheep roamed all over the place. It was considered the house-owner's problem to keep the sheep out, hence all gates must be securely fastened. There was a small gate at the side of the cattle grid for the use of pedestrians. Imagine our surprise when we received a telephone call one day from a very frantic parent, who lived near the hostel. It went something like this: 'Is that Mrs Pratt?' to which I answered in the affirmative; 'Have you got a big, light-coloured dog called Kelly?' to which I again answered 'Yes'. 'Could you come and collect her, please? She's here in my kitchen where my three young children are playing with her and feeding her biscuits. I'm scared and I can't go in to them, although the children assure me that she is safe and will not bite.' Someone must have left the side gate open and Kelly wandered out. The children, all under seven years of age, took Kelly home with them. When we called to bring her home, the children were sad to see her leave.

SOME BULLMASTIFF ADVENTURES

The next story was written by Steve Nicholas in *National Dog*, an Australian publication, in June 1990 and it relates to an Australian-born Bullmastiff bitch, Jackie, whelped in Canberra, the capital of Australia. "Jackie was whelped on October 2nd 1983. Her sire, Lombardy Taurus, carried in him fine old English blood, and her dam, whelped in Victoria, also carried English blood from some outstanding kennels, including Pitmans. Jackie was the smallest of the litter and the last

The Bullmastiff is gentle and trustworthy with children.

to be sold. She was purchased by a gentleman from Sydney and little is known of her life around that time, though it would seem that her first months were relatively normal, and there was little or no intention to show Jackie. At the age of eight months she was, for reasons unknown, sold. Her new owners already owned an assortment of dogs, mainly with Bull Terrier blood crossed with various other breeds and, apart from their love of motor cycles and the gangs that go with them, loved to hunt wild pigs. It would appear that Jackie excelled at this 'sport'. Her food intake was reduced so that she would stay lean and be able to hunt more. When not hunting she was tied to a makeshift kennel in the rear garden of the house. In these formative years of her life, apart from the trials and tribulations that she had to endure, she also had to contend with nature, and in due course she was mated and had young.

"Jackie formed a bond with one of the children, a nineteen-year-old boy. One day, however, when Jackie and the young man were together and she was not restrained, the young man's father decided he would issue some summary jurisdiction on the young man for some misdemeanour. The father, a large, powerful man, approached his son with the intention of dispensing some discipline. It isn't known whether the father's fist actually came into contact with the boy, but Jackie decided very quickly that in order to protect her friend, attack was the only course. With speed and power she lunged at the man and caught his arm in her powerful jaws and bit hard. This was no game of grab and tug, far from that – the conflict was serious, and Jackie held her grip for quite some time. Her victim, obviously in some degree of pain, began to hit her head and face with a large piece of wood to try and make her release her grip, which she eventually did.

"She was retained by these people as a hunting dog in less than desirable circumstances until March 1985, when she was advertised in the Pets section of a local Sydney newspaper. Don Butler, who had read about the breed, saw the advertisement and decided to have a look at the animal. Don described how when he first saw her, she was very lean, and the scars on her head and legs from the wild pigs and fights, made her look a very sorry sight. Also, she was missing a lower canine, a result of the belting with the block of wood. He recalls how his first impression of the house put him off somewhat, but negotiations were completed and she was taken home. Jackie soon settled into her new home, which was at that time a villa home, with only a very small garden. Jackie, however, did not mind, as this environment was far better than the one she had been used to. In her new life she has been bred and she has been shown. She gained her Australian

Championship, being shown from March 1986 to June 1986. She was never refused a challenge certificate (scars and lower canine missing) and went on to win best open in Utility Group at the County of Cumberland Anzac Day Show on April 25th 1986, under Victorian judge Rosemary D'Agostin – much to the disgust of the Boxer and Dobermann owners in her group, who labelled her "Scarface"! Jackie was entered in the Sydney Royal Easter Show in April 1987 and 1988 and she won challenge bitch and best of breed both years. She has now produced seven Australian champions (to 1989) and she is a lovely healthy girl, much loved, who has turned six years old. Jackie is Australian Champion Vanetta Cindy, owned by the Bullpower Kennels of Sydney."

Here is another story written in the same publication by Andrew Burt. "We were delighted when Kelly arrived! A beautiful little red ball with a cuddly black face and dark, inky eyes. The search for a quality bitch Bullmastiff puppy had been a long one. There were very few litters at the time in Victoria, let alone other Australian states. I chose Kelly from photos of a New Zealand litter bred by Christine and Barry Powley. The mating combined excellent Victorian lines with some UK stock. We were very grateful to the Powleys for letting us have such a lovely puppy. Kelly slotted very easily into home life and very quickly established her position both as the head of our family, and at the head of the bed as often as she could. She was reasonably easily trained and we excitedly embarked upon her show career at the 1977 Bullmastiff Club Open Parade. She won best baby puppy in parade, and followed this with best puppy in show at the Club's Championship Show in October. Kelly took her first big CC at a Club point score show in excellent company while still a puppy. We were thrilled! Kelly was showing indications of developing into a quality bitch and also she had become an important and valuable family member.

"The following February in 1978, Kelly was stolen. She was twelve months old and in season at the time. It was a terribly traumatic experience for our family and I think the aspect that upset us most was the not knowing. We had no clues as to her whereabouts except that a tracking Standard Poodle was able to track Kelly through a gate we never used, to the side of the road where the scent disappeared. We could only assume that she had been put into a car. Many valuable lessons were learnt that day. Bullmastiffs have always been valued for cross breeding by pig hunters, but most reputable Bullmastiff breeders did not sell animals to anyone they felt may use the dog for this purpose. We had very secure gates and fences but no locks. I had also been advertising a puppy from Perth for a friend, and given out our address several times over the previous weekend. However, lessons well learnt did not help our heartbreak at the time. Many people in Victorian dogdom knew of Kelly's theft and we were lucky to have someone spreading the word through hunting circles. In September that year, after we had finally begun to accept that Kelly was gone for good, I received an anonymous phone call that gave us new hope. I was led to believe that Kelly was on a property at Beenleigh, Queensland. The Melbourne Police said nothing could be done unless I was prepared to fly to Queensland. Arrangements were quick. Queensland Police were contacted and I flew out of Melbourne leaving midway through the Royal and my university exams. A day later, excluding the lengthy details, I found our Kelly. To this day I am extremely grateful to the Queensland Police and the members of the Queensland dog fraternity who were involved in Kelly's recovery. Amazingly, Kelly was not really affected by her experience but I am quite sure she could have related some spellbinding stories of her missing eight months. She had two small scars, she had whelped a litter and was supposedly five weeks in whelp to an Irish Wolfhound, but thankfully no puppies eventuated. Despite all that had happened, she still had her puppy disposition and love of life and everyone in it.

"Within a month Kelly was back in full bloom and she won best in show at the Bullmastiff Club of Victoria Championship show in October that year. Australian Ch. Arabella of Arapeti (Imp NZ) had an enviable show career, including wins at Melbourne and Adelaide Royals and two breed

Specialties. She was Victorian Bitch of the Year three times. Kelly never produced pedigree puppies as she was eventually spayed due to a continuing infection that may or may not have resulted from her time in Queensland. In April 1982 she was put to sleep following a severe illness. It was a hard decision for our family but we were determined that once she began to suffer it must come to an end quickly. Kelly gave our family over five years of untiring fun and happiness. Her life had certainly been rich in experience and we are proud that Kelly was always such a good ambassador for the breed. She leaves a legacy of fond memories not only with our family, but with her many, many friends who have experienced a wet lick of her tongue, a belt of her wagging tail, a laughing glint from her eye, or the weight of her great body sitting on their feet."

OWNING A BULLMASTIFF

What of today? Would-be owners are advised that if they have a Bullmastiff it is not just another dog, but a member of the family. You don't own a Bullmastiff; a Bullmastiff owns you. A full-grown Bullmastiff will take as much, or as little, exercise as you are willing to give. All things being equal, they prefer their exercise on the back seat of anyone's car. The average dogs run their lives by the clock; not Bullmastiffs. They will take their exercise when you are ready. If conditions are such that you are unable to take your dog out, the Bullmastiff will understand and will look at you with those dark brown eyes and you know the dog is saying, "What is wrong? Tell me about it and we'll both feel better." The strange thing is; you do talk about it, and you do feel better.

To many of us, Bullmastiffs are 'people dogs'. They have an uncanny feeling about people and will never waste time on anyone who doesn't like dogs. Many years ago we had, as I have mentioned before, a bitch named Kelly, who was known and loved by people of all ages. Anyone who came into the house was given a hearty welcome. One day, we had a visitor who backed away from her. In turn, Kelly left the room. The man said: 'Is your dog safe? She looks as if she could eat me.' We assured him that Kelly was very reliable and would never attack anyone. A few days later that man was found hanging in a nearby wood. We always thought that Kelly was able to sense something about him that made her feel uneasy. Although a moderately large dog the Bullmastiff is also a very quiet beast who will not bark unless there is a just reason for doing so, and no one should attempt to teach a Bullmastiff to 'guard'. Until about eighteen months of age it is quite possible that the owners may never hear the dog bark, especially during the hours of daylight.

Few Bullmastiffs have been really successful in the Obedience ring. Why, you may ask. A good Bullmastiff likes to please the owners *but,* and it's a big *but,* it must be on the dog's terms. Constant repetition is boring to an intelligent dog. You throw a stick and the dog brings it back to you. You throw it again and there is no response except a worried expression as if your dog is saying 'I've just returned that stick; why have you thrown it away again. Am I to understand that you don't want it?' A friend, Janet McKnight, had a lovely dog named Bobby, who accompanied her everywhere, even when she went shopping. At the command, Stay, Bobby would sit outside the shop waiting for his mistress to return. He wasn't chained and didn't move until Janet collected him after finishing her shopping. Everyone in the neighbourhood knew Bobby and eventually Janet was persuaded to take him along to Obedience classes. The dog was happy meeting other dogs on a weekly basis and he seemed to enjoy the various exercises, even though his attempts were probably much slower than any other of the dogs. Then came the big day when he had to perform 'Down five minutes, handler out of sight'. Everyone assured Janet that Bobby would pass this test with flying colours. Didn't he sit patiently outside the shops, while she was inside, out of sight? The owners placed their dogs in a long line and then left the room. There was a small window through which observers could watch the dogs. After all the handlers had left the room, Bobby stood up, looked around, and made for the door. He was the first one to break position. That was the end of Obedience classes for him.

THE FORGOTTEN KING OF GUARD DOGS

Colonel David Hancock provides the final contribution to this chapter on Character. He has had many years experience with dogs and has written a book, *Dogs as Companions,* published in 1980. "Safe, silent and secure. Our intruder alarm needs no mechanical maintenance, can be placed on duty all night without relief; and possesses a built-in night-vision capability, has an innate IFF (Identification Friend or Foe) indicator, can operate for 24 hour periods without power supply, and lasts at least 10 years before needing a replacement. What a product for any security company salesman to peddle! And what is that product – a guard dog, and in particular the breed called Bullmastiffs. But why Bullmastiffs? Why not Alsatians, Elkhounds, or Airedales for that matter. The difference is that the Bullmastiffs were intentionally and specifically bred for such duties. They were the 'Gamekeeper's Dog'. Just as the poacher needed a Lurcher to locate, chase, kill and retrieve game, silently and swiftly, so the gamekeeper required a powerful, obedient dog to locate, seize and detain the poacher. Not a task for a light, racy, noisy, fidgety, ill-disciplined dog, but the strong silent type, able on command to knock down, and then hold down, a healthy, fit young countryman, perhaps after tracking him, or quietly observing him acting illegally for a while.

"Having decided the requirement, the desired product was then tailor-made for the job. A cross between the Bulldog, tough, tenacious, fuss-less, brave and with silent self-reliance, and the Mastiff, massively powerful, trustworthy, fearsome in appearance, but stable by nature, loyal and immensely brave, produced the Bullmastiff, 27 inches at the withers, some ten stones (140 lbs) of hefty guard-dog. From these carefully selected ancestors, specially purpose-bred, came a strapping, utterly fearless, superbly proportioned, imposing looking animal, combining the massive size and sheer pugnacity of appearance of the age-old, beautifully tempered Mastiff, bred with the famed courage and proven endurance of the renowned Bulldog. These two famous breeds gave the modern Bullmastiff three priceless qualities, unique in combination in one dog; superb temperament, even-tempered, level-headed, magnanimous and never excitable; a silent, steadfast and almost arrogant bearing; and, most important of all, the instinct to pin the quarry rather than bite.

"The powerful Bullmastiff doesn't savage its target or "worry" the arm of a standing "wanted" man; the dog has the strength and the inherited impulse to pin the victim to the floor or a wall. Another asset not to be undervalued is the considerable deterrent value of the Bullmastiff's sheer size, splendidly pugnacious black-masked face and impressive, almost regally impassive composure – a dog who really looks the part. Yet this formidable dog adores children, never loses its temper and tolerates endless teasing and petty abuse. Bullmastiffs are responsive to training, intelligent and faithful by nature, can track as well as guard, and are a comforting companion.

"Having been employed as a guard-dog in such widely separated situations as the Mau-Mau emergency in Kenya, in the Kimberley diamond mines in South Africa, and on John D. Rockefeller's huge country estate in New York State, the Bullmastiff is now used mainly by discerning private owners as a companion/guard. Other breeds seem to be favoured as professional guard dogs – Alsatians (German Shepherd Dogs), Dobermann Pinschers, Rottweilers and Giant Schnauzers. The last three breeds, however, have uncertain temperaments, require a very firm hand and, by instinct, "savage" their quarry. The Alsatian, when well-bred, well-trained and kept in suitable circumstances, has many admirable qualities. But Alsatians used as guard-dogs act, not surprisingly, as a converted sheep-dog would be expected to. They are an ill-used breed in many ways. Suffering from sudden post-war popularity, they have not always been wisely bred, and are frequently owned by quite the wrong people. The very small number of incidents of people being savaged by Alsatians has received adverse publicity. The restless pacing, ceaselessly barking and frenziedly snarling caged 'Alsatian-type' guard-dogs in second-hand car dealers' or scrap merchants' yards give this breed a very doubtful public image. The wolf-like silhouette probably sets the seal for those already thinking ill of them. The fact is that it is a sheep-dog's instinct to 'rush in and nip', or pretend to nip, and even with Alsatians which have never seen a sheep, this trait has to be disciplined.

"I suspect that for professional guard-dog duties, by security firms, in prisons, on country estates and in burglar and vandal-prone premises, the Bullmastiff would be extensively employed, if only the breed's qualities were known. Yet sadly, quite unsuitable dogs are being used by ill-advised people. But who wants to be sued because a so-called guard-dog has savaged straying adventurous children? Who wants to be taken to court over an endlessly barking 'security dog'? The temperament, the instinct and the physical impression of a guard-dog are the vital components for success in the job. The Bullmastiff doesn't snap or nip and very rarely barks; can track as well as guard; is easy to train and control and tolerates children more than perhaps any other breed. On duty a Bullmastiff does not savage prey, but silently and effectively 'detains' it. That great powerful head with the ferocious scowling black mask and the lasting impression of sheer physical power makes the Bullmastiff a formidable, commanding figure for any wrong-doer to confront. A loyal, faithful, even-tempered, noble breed, they make superb companion-guards and do not have that restless energy which demands a vast amount of exercise. When all is said and done about the various breeds available as guard-dogs, the Bullmastiff is the professional, bred for the part. After all, who would employ a shepherd as a night-watchman when a security guard is available. And which would you prefer to be guarded by, a lion or a wolf? The Bullmastiff is the lion of the dog world: massive, arrogant, powerful and brave – a truly underrated, undervalued king among dogs."

Chapter Three

THE BULLMASTIFF PUPPY

IS A BULLMASTIFF THE RIGHT BREED FOR YOU?

So, you have decided that you would like a Bullmastiff puppy. Before you proceed any further, stop and think carefully. If, after a few months, you decide that the dog is going to be too big, or is costing too much to feed properly, what are you going to do? Are you going to foist the poor thing on "Bullmastiff Welfare" or try to find the puppy a new home? New homes for large puppies are not easy to come by. A Bullmastiff puppy will weigh about one to one-and-a-quarter pounds at birth. In the first four or five weeks the puppy may increase in weight between three and four ounces per day, and at seven or eight weeks may weigh eighteen pounds or more. Can you afford the good food which is necessary if the puppy is to grow into a sound healthy adult of ninety pounds or more? You can? Then what is the next step?

CHOOSING THE RIGHT STOCK

Before you decide on one particular puppy you must try to see as many adult Bullmastiffs as you can. Look in the canine press and find out where the dog shows are. If you can attend a breed club show it will be all the better for you. Talk to the breeders and exhibitors and listen carefully. If possible, take notes. Some breeders will try to persuade you that other breeders are not good, but

Bullmaster Indiana, owned and bred by the Bullmaster kennel. Think carefully before you take on the responsibility of owning a puppy who will grow into a big, powerful dog.

Aust. Ch. Bulwaren The Highwayman, bred by Mr and Mrs E. Van Blommestein, owned by Mrs P. Quinn.
The male Bullmastiff will be bigger and heavier than the female, and so it is essential to establish your authority over him from an early stage.

you must not get involved. Sales talk can often persuade people to buy rubbish. A good breeder should be able to produce litters of puppies which are very similar in type and conformation. A line of champions (usually printed in red) on a pedigree does not always denote good bloodlines. Look at closely-related stock; the family pattern should be there.

Look at the general type of the adults. Have they got good heads, with dark, clear eyes; good mouths with strong even teeth; good ear carriage; have they got a reasonable slope of shoulders; are their front legs straight, finishing off with good, round feet; are the backs reasonably short and level; have they got a fair bend of stifle with the hind legs finishing off with round cat feet; are the tails set on high, coming down to the hocks; are their nails black? If you can answer yes to most of these questions, watch them on the move. Movement should be free and easy and neither the front nor rear feet should cross. Are the dogs friendly? If you find a breed line which fits most of these points, then you could take a chance on a puppy. Beware of the breeders who tell you that their puppies are show winners. All that honest breeders can say is that their puppies are as well-bred and as well-reared as is humanly possible. Winning in the show ring is an extra bonus. Most of us have seen our puppies change as they develop – ugly ducklings became swans and promising cygnets became ugly ducks.

Ch. Bryany Brunette, bred by Mr C. Taylor, owned by Ray and Alex Goodlad. If you choose a bitch, you will have to cope with her seasonal cycle.

MALE OR FEMALE?

The next decision is very important; do you want a male or a female? For some, the obvious choice would be a male. The reason given would be that a dog doesn't come into season twice a year like the average female. This is a fallacy. The average male is in season all the year round. If he gets the scent of a female in season, he may go off his food and he may spend the hours of darkness howling like a lost soul. If he can get out he may pursue the trail of any female. On the other hand, a female becomes very devoted to her family and seldom tries to get away. When she is in season she can be confined away from contact with any males. A regular dosing with veterinary deodorant tablets will help to neutralise the smell. A note of caution, however. If you intend to mate the female, these tablets must not be given for at least three or four days before the expected date of mating. If the female is kept indoors, there are various items of canine clothing sold at good pet shops, which will help avoid staining of carpets etc.

COLOUR

Bullmastiffs come in any shade of brindle, fawn or red. What colour will you choose? The fawn is very attractive with a black muzzle, dark ears and dark eyes. From experience, the fawns have a

*TOP LEFT: Ch. Todomas
Tamara, owned and bred by
Tom Massey. The fawn-
coloured Bullmastiff with its
striking black muzzle.
J&B Phoenix Photography.*

*ABOVE: Am. Ch. Mister US
Music Man, owned by Bill
Underwood and David and
Janet Morris: Number One
Bullmastiff (all systems) 1990-
1992. The red-coloured
Bullmastiff has a rich gloss to
its coat.*

*LEFT: Murbisa Chasing
Rainbows, aged ten months. A
well-marked brindle is an
impressive looking animal.*

thick, coarse coat with a fluffy undercoat. They need constant grooming to get rid of loose hairs and to get a shine on the coat. The reds seem to be finer in coat, but the black muzzle and dark ears do not show up quite as much as they do in the fawns. There appears to be a gloss in the red coat that responds to a little less grooming than that of the fawn coat. What of the brindle? Having worked my way through a breeding programme of fawns to reds to brindles, my favourite is the latter. A well-marked brindle, ranging from a light fawn background with black stripes, to a dark red background with black stripes, complete with black mask and velvety black ears, presents a picture of a very handsome animal. Again, from experience, many brindles have a finer coat and this lies closer to the body, giving the impression of lighter bone. If showing is your intention and you are willing to accept a challenge, have a brindle.

PET OR SHOW DOG?
Seeing a puppy of six weeks, it is difficult to imagine the future development. This is a breed which doesn't follow a set pattern. Some grow upwards quickly and appear to be all legs. Others grow slowly and evenly. The head does not finish developing until a Bullmastiff is two to three years old. How then can we decide which puppy we will have? Look at puppies and adults from constantly placed bloodlines. Good stock will be placed under all-rounders and breed specialists, no matter who the handler is. A puppy from a consistently winning bloodline could be a safe bet; but expect to pay a higher price for it. No breeder can profess that a puppy will be a Champion – only that the puppy is as well bred and as well reared as is humanly possible. The rest is in the lap of the gods. A pet puppy has faults which can be seen quite early: a crank tail; very pale blue eyes, which will almost certainly become light eyes; straight stifles; white feet and excess white on the chest; lack of the essential black muzzle, or even the presence of a muzzle which is blue or brown. Do not believe any breeder who tells you that the faults will change as the puppy develops. *They will not.* Whatever your decision you make, love the puppy for the puppy's own sake and you will receive love and pleasure in return.

CHOOSING A BREEDER
You have decided on the sex and the colour of your puppy. The final decision is most important – choosing the breeder.

If you can, ask one or two breeders if you can see their dogs. Without making it too obvious, check that any outdoor stock is housed in clean and comfortable quarters. Are all the dogs clean and healthy? It is also important to note how the dogs respond to you. If they are aggressive or withdrawn, this may indicate behavioural problems. If they are friendly towards you, this will give you an opportunity to look at them more closely. Are the eyes dark? Are the eyelids clean or are they covered in mucus? The breeder may say that the dog's eyes have dirt in them, or that the dog has been out in the car and refuses to travel unless the windows are wound down. Check on the colour and condition of the coats. The coats should be shiny and close to the body. What are the feet like? Are they cat-like with short, black, toenails?

So far so good! The premises seem clean and comfortable and all the dogs seem clean and healthy, but there are still a few points to consider. Here are a few questions you might ask:-
1. I've never had a Bullmastiff before. If I find that I cannot cope, will you take the puppy back?
2. Do you offer a guarantee of good health?
3. Are the dogs X-rayed for HD?
4. How long have you been breeding Bullmastiffs? How many litters do you breed each year?
5. Are there any problems in the breed? (Do not believe the breeder who says "No".)
6. Can I see some of your pedigrees? (Try to get the breeder to talk about some of the dogs on the

pedigrees. If they have a genuine interest in their breeding programme, they should be able to talk freely about the first two or three generations.)

7. What points do you breed for?

8. Do your dogs receive regular boosters etc.?

9. What do you charge for a potential show specimen and what do you charge for a pet? (Prices vary considerably and you may have to pay a high price for a puppy from a good kennel. A cheap puppy may prove to be expensive in the long run, because the breeders are anxious to sell it.)

10. When are you hoping to have a litter? Will you contact me please?

CHOOSING THE PUPPY

If you have decided which bloodlines satisfy your investigations, try to see one or two litters. You will already have seen the sires or the dams; or you will have seen some of their brothers and sisters. When you look at the litters see how the puppies compare with each other. There should not be a wide variation in size between the puppies in a litter. The odd puppy may be a little bigger than the rest, or one a little smaller. If the eyes are open, try to see if the eyes are a very dark blue and the eye-lids are clean. Dark blue eyes usually turn into dark brown eyes. If the eye-lids are crusted, it could be the result of a minor injury, or the onset of entropion, which is the turning in of the margin of the eyelid..

   It's always difficult to assess the milk teeth. In the early weeks it is sufficient to see that the teeth are relatively even and edge-to-edge. Usually, the under jaw continues to grow long after the upper jaw has ceased, and what was almost a scissor bite can finish up badly undershot. Some people are tempted to take a chance on a puppy which appears slightly overshot in the hope that the under jaw continues to grow. If this does not happen, an overshot mouth is penalised more heavily than an undershot mouth. At the beginning the head may appear to be quite plain; the ears may be erratic and the muzzle a little long. Look at the muzzle carefully. Is it the same width under the eyes as it is at the end? If it is, there is every chance that when the cheeks develop, the head will be good. A short muzzle in a very young puppy will look even shorter when the cheeks develop. Run the tail between your index finger and your thumb. It should be straight from root to tail. A short

Mme Berthou pictured with a litter of Bullmastiff puppies in France. The litter should be evenly matched in size, and the puppies should be clean, lively and inquisitive.

When choosing a puppy it helps if you can see other close relatives, as this will give you an idea how the litter will turn out.

Oddrock Chuck Berry, aged 19 weeks. Growth is very rapid in the first six months of a Bullmastiff's life.

tail, or a crank tail, may be heavily penalised in the show ring. Do not believe any breeder who tells you that gentle massage will smooth away any kink. It will not. A crank tail will always be a crank tail. Try to look at the puppy standing four-square. The front legs should be straight and the hind legs should show a fair bend of stifle. Again, do not believe any breeder who tells you that a straight stifle will disappear as the puppy develops. A straight stifle will always be a straight stifle and looks worse as the puppy grows. Whatever the colour you have chosen, avoid any puppy with an excess of white. Slight white markings on the chin or feet may grow out, but you cannot rely on it. Whatever the colour, the muzzle must be black, tapering off below the eyes. The black appears again round the eyes. The ears must be darker in colour than the body colouring; the darker they are, the better.

Watch the puppies play together. They should be reasonably steady. Avoid any puppies which tremble or seem uncertain of their movement. Try to attract their attention by moving your finger. Failure to respond may indicate eye problems. If you have your heart set on one particular puppy, place your hand gently on its back and draw your fingers together. If the puppy is in good condition, you will find that the skin is very loose and seems to come away from the body. When the skin is released, it should return close to the body – smooth and shiny. A fluffy, woolly coat may indicate worms or other health problems. Another indication of worms is a pot belly. Once you have decided which puppy you would like, you must arrange with the breeder about price etc. You must not collect the puppy until at least eight weeks of age. If the registration papers are not at hand it is advisable to have a document drawn up, and properly witnessed, to say that you have agreed to purchase the puppy whose name has been applied for. Do not hand over the full purchase price until you receive the registration papers. If there are conditions attached to the sale of the puppy, be sure that you understand them. I would always advise buyers to buy a puppy without any strings attached. The conditions may include one puppy out of the first litter, if it is a bitch. What happens when there is only one puppy? Think carefully!

PREPARING FOR YOUR PUPPY
If you have a garden, steps must be taken to see that it is secure. A Bullmastiff puppy grows very quickly and during this time becomes very adventurous. A 3 ft (100 cm) fence will contain a three-to-four month old, but it will soon be useless. The puppy will either climb over it or dig underneath it. You must erect either a strong wooden fence, or a galvanised wire mesh fence with strong metal supports, at least 5 ft (150 cm) high. The base can either be buried in the soil or concreted in place. If there is a gate, it must be strong and rigid, and held securely by two bolts or padlocks. If it is a big garden, it is a good idea to have an outdoor kennel with a run attached. The run can be approximately 10 ft (350 cm) wide, 15 ft (425 cm) long, 5 ft (150 cm) high. Again, the base must be buried or concreted and the gate must be secure. The run can be paved or concreted, so that it can be kept clean.

If the puppy is to spend most of the early weeks indoors, do not allow play in a room where an "accident" can ruin the carpet. The kitchen, where the floor is covered with tiles or linoleum, is an ideal place for a puppy. The kitchen door also provides quick and easy access to the garden. If you have sufficient space, buy one of the large dog crates and put the puppy's bed in there. The puppy will get used to going in there and it will provide a safe place during the night, or if you are out during the day. The crate must be away from all draughts. At one end of the crate you can put down sheets of newspaper; no self-respecting puppy will soil the bed. During the day, when someone is in the house, you could have a piece of newspaper behind the kitchen door – a prelude to going outdoors.

Inside the crate, the puppy can have a big woolly toy, something to cuddle up to. Do not let the puppy have small balls, small rubber toys or small bones in the crate, for one of these may be swallowed and the result could be fatal. If you have an old woollen jumper or some old woollen socks, you can stuff them inside each other and stitch them up securely. The gate of the crate must be left open when there is someone in the house, but the rest of the time it must be closed. In time the puppy will grow to accept the crate as a personal "den" and will go in there quite happily. The puppy will be safe from harm and your furniture will be safe from damage. Near the crate, you can have a tray or a plastic mat on which will be a water bowl and a feeding dish. The water must be fresh daily and the food dish must be removed after every meal. Cleanliness is essential and all scraps of food must be removed from the surrounding area. You will have agreed with the breeder the type of food your puppy is used to. You must have a supply in hand, or arrange to buy some from the breeder. It is essential that the puppy does not encounter too many changes when moving to your home. It will be a traumatic experience anyway. The puppy may be leaving behind litter mates and, certainly, mother, and may be moving outdoors after having lived indoors, or vice versa. Be prepared for a few days of unrest, and try to stay calm, cool and collected.

Before you go to collect the puppy, make arrangements with your vet for an examination. Depending on this, the puppy may be inoculated if the vet agrees. This first examination may save a lot of heartache later. The vet will advise about worming, or any other treatment that may be necessary, or may see problems which escaped your notice. Puppies, like small children, change from day to day. It is better to be safe than sorry.

COLLECTING THE PUPPY

The great day arrives. Before it ends you will be the proud owner of a unique puppy – a Bullmastiff. Do a last-minute check to see that the garden is secure; the bed is prepared in the kitchen; there is a good supply of the puppy's usual food; there is a good supply of newspaper. Everything and everybody is prepared to receive the new member of the family. If at all possible, take a companion with you when you go for the puppy. One of you can concentrate on the driving and the other on the puppy. The puppy can travel in a large, cardboard box, lined with thick layers of newspaper and a piece of blanket. Take along a few extra pieces of blanket and a roll of kitchen paper. You may not need them, but be prepared for any eventuality. Check the puppy as carefully as you can, to see that this is the one which you chose. If you are not happy about the puppy, you must say so. Before you leave with the puppy, be sure that you have a copy of the pedigree and the registration certificate. If the certificate is not there, you must get a written statement that it will be forwarded as soon as it is available. If the breeder is well-known and respected, there should not be any further problems. If you have any doubts, do not pay the full price for the puppy. Sign an agreement that you will pay the balance when you receive the registration certificate. On the journey home you must not let the puppy out of the car. If you do, the puppy may try to run away and could prove difficult to capture. Also an eight-week-old will not have been inoculated and will be susceptible to infection.

INTRODUCING THE FAMILY

The first essential when you arrive home is to allow the puppy to relieve itself. If it is light and the weather is fine, go in the garden or the outer run. Give the puppy time to run around the place. When the necessary has been done, give lots of praise – "Good dog" – and bring the puppy indoors. The puppy must be allowed to make the first move towards any member of the family, *and must not be crowded or picked up by children.* The puppy may be very excitable until the family becomes familiar and could so easily be dropped from small fingers. An eight-week-old puppy may weigh between 17 lbs (8 kg) and 22 lbs (10 kg), making quite a handful for anyone to pick up, and if dropped, this may cause injury or set up a fear of being handled. The puppy, having explored the kitchen, will begin to slow down. Now is the time to offer a drink of clean water. When a puppy has been weaned, vets advise against the use of cow's milk as it upsets the digestive system. Introduce the puppy to the bed inside the crate, and the woolly toy. The puppy, who is tired after a long journey, may settle down for a few minutes. If this happens, tell the family that this rest must not be disturbed. Now is the time to prepare some food. It is most important to stress that the food must be the same as that on which the puppy has been weaned. If it is a proprietary brand, follow the instructions as given. If it is a food which must be moistened, beef or chicken gravy may improve the flavour and make it more appetising.

The puppy, on wakening, must be put out of doors at once. Nine times out of ten, the puppy will urinate. Put the food down and leave the puppy to eat. Here it is of vital importance to tell the family about the two basic rules of puppy training. A pup must not be disturbed either when sleeping or when eating. Once it is obvious that the puppy has eaten enough, pick up the dish and put the puppy outdoors to urinate and defecate. There you have both rules. The puppy must not be disturbed when eating or sleeping and must be put outdoors immediately on waking and on finishing eating. The latter may seem a little tedious at the outset; but believe me – if you stick at it, the puppy will soon realise why this is being done. You will, of course, give praise when the puppy obliges; you may even give a little treat. Thus, what could be a monotonous chore finishes with good feelings on both sides. The puppy, on coming back indoors, may want to sleep. Put the puppy into the bed you have prepared, thus establishing that this is the puppy's own place. If you have small children, tell them that the puppy must not play just after being fed, because it may make the puppy sick. Remember that the first few days are a learning process for puppy and family alike. There must be one set of rules and everyone must obey those rules. The average Bullmastiff puppy soon learns what is and what is not allowed, even while, like a child, attempting to break the rules; but everyone in the house must be firm. It may seem hard at the outset, but it is worth it in the long run. If we are honest, we do not like naughty children or naughty puppies. The tone of voice should be sufficient. A sharp "No!" will carry far more weight than "You are naughty. You mustn't do that."

THE FIRST NIGHT
When you decide that it is bed-time, allow the puppy to play for a while. If a drink is given, it must be a small one. Put the puppy outdoors for the last time and prepare the bed. As I have said before, the ideal situation is at the far end of a large dog-crate. It can be made of plastic or wood. If funds are low, a strong cardboard box will suffice. The sides must be high enough to keep out the draught, but low enough for the puppy to get into. You must provide a soft woolly toy, or "what have you" – something that will act as a substitute mother or sibling, something to cuddle up with. Some people put a clock with a loud tick by the side of the crate, on the assumption that the loud tick will resemble the mother's heart beat. I have never tried it.

One thing I do know: there is no fool-proof method of making a puppy sleep in a new home. You must be prepared for one or more sleepless nights. The puppy who is well fed and relaxed, in a warm and comfortable bed, may sleep for some time. Try to ensure that this sleep is not disturbed. When you get up in the morning, put the puppy outside immediately. If the paper near the entry to the crate, or behind the kitchen door, has been soiled, take it out; clean the floor with mild antiseptic/disinfectant and lay down a fresh supply of clean paper. If you keep the crate or kennel clean, the puppy will accept that as the norm and will try to keep it that way.

FEEDING
You will have received a diet sheet from your breeder and you will have laid in a stock of food. Do not try to change the diet in the first few days. This can have disastrous results for the puppy.

Most breeders nowadays feed "complete foods". As the name implies, the foods are complete; they are balanced in every detail; which means you do not use any additives! An excess of calcium, for example, does not make for good bone growth. In many cases it causes problems with the normal development of the bone. Try to remember that the Bullmastiff is a slow developer and if you attempt to speed up growth, you are storing up problems for later years. Feed small meals at regular intervals. Do not feed straight from the fridge. As your puppy grows, increase the amount in each meal, but always remember: it is better to underfeed than overfeed. A fat puppy is *not* a healthy puppy. The sad thing is many owners, breeders and judges cannot differentiate between fat and real substance. How often does a judge write of a dog in good, hard condition, "fails in substance"?

When the puppy is really settled you can provide cooked fish, cooked cow's heart or cooked liver as an occasional treat. We are lucky, as we can still obtain cow's tripes from the abattoir. These are bought on the day the beasts are killed and the tripe is cut into small pieces, boxed and frozen. You can either wash the tripe before cutting, or after freezing and thawing out. It is fed raw. From time to time scrambled eggs and cheese are given as supplements. Lamb's liver is cooked slowly in the microwave. Biscuits are always fed dry. The larger biscuits help to develop the jaws and clean the teeth. If you can manage it, buy a marrow bone from time to time. Again, it will help develop the jaws and, if you can saw through it, the puppy will love the marrow bone jelly. Whatever food you use, it must always be fresh. If it is a food which needs soaking, be sure to allow sufficient time for the moisture to soak in. A dog who is getting the right food will be lively and happy, the coat will shine, and the skin will be loose.

GROWTH RATE

This varies from puppy to puppy and the dogs usually grow quicker than the bitches. It quite often happens that once the puppies are weaned, the smaller ones begin to catch up. Unfortunately, it is not always easy to weigh a Bullmastiff after weaning. You can weigh yourself on the bathroom scales and then weigh yourself with the puppy. It is worth a try. The following rough guide has been in use for many years. It is an estimate of what weight may be gained and not of what weight should be gained.

Weight at:

21 days	6 lbs or	3.0 kg
28 days	8 lbs or	3.5 kg
35 days	10 lbs or	4.5 kg
42 days	12 lbs or	5.5 kg
49 days	16 lbs or	7.5 kg
60 days	21 lbs or	9.5 kg
91 days	37 lbs or	17.5 kg

Average weights vary with different bloodlines. As long as you can see that the puppy is continuing to gain weight steadily, there should be no cause for alarm.

EXERCISE

Before you can begin to think about exercise, you must get your puppy accustomed to a collar. If you are lucky, you may have a friend whose puppy has grown out of the first size collar and a quick wash or wipe down with an antiseptic solution makes it ready for use. A soft leather collar does not present as many problems as a chain-link choker. If the puppy wears the latter, the links may get hooked up on trees and shrubs in the garden. The chain-link choker does last longer, as its usage depends on getting it over the head. You will need two or three changes in the size of the collar or the choker before the puppy is full grown. Once the collar is on, the puppy may begin to scratch in an attempt to remove the offending article. A few minutes at a time is the answer. When the puppy stops scratching you can leave the collar on for longer periods, until you can leave the collar on all day. At this point I must stress my preference for a leather collar. If, for any reason, you need to restrain the puppy, a leather collar is much easier on the hands than a chain-link choker. It is also easier to adjust a leather collar to the puppy's ever-increasing neck size.

The next stage may, or may not, be a difficult one. Attach the lead to the collar. Some puppies may at this stage develop the role of a "bucking bronco", rearing on their hind legs and pulling in all directions. Please be patient! Do not scold the puppy! Do not attempt to move forward with the puppy in tow. Talk to the puppy in a soft voice, giving reassurance that all is well. It may take two or three attempts before the puppy will accept the lead attached to the collar. Once the puppy is settled, you can try to walk a few yards. Again, patience is the criterion. The puppy may try to run on in front; may cross backwards and forwards; may even sit down. Whatever happens, do not

Ch. Maxstoke Bassey, owned and bred by Colin and Mary Jones.
It is very important not to over-exercise your Bullmastiff in the first twelve months of its life.

scold, do not tug the lead. Before you know it, the puppy will be walking on the lead. For the first two or three months, a few yards, two or three times a day, will be ample. You must remember that before reaching twelve months of age, your puppy will be much bigger than adult dogs of other breeds, *but,* and it is a big *but,* your Bullmastiff will still be a puppy. Resist the temptation to take your puppy for long walks, as this will do far more harm than good. At six months you can go a little further but at any appearance of fatigue, either turn back or rest for a while. Your dog will probably finish growing in height from fifteen to eighteen months, but the body and head may take much longer. Try to remember that too much exercise for a growing puppy or junior can have disastrous results for which there is no cure. When fully grown, a Bullmastiff will take as much exercise as you are willing to give but, on sighting a car, is partial to a ride on the back seat. For the most part, Bullmastiffs are wonderful car travellers.

CAR TRAVEL

You will have made an appointment with your vet for an examination. This will be the puppy's second car journey. Put a piece of blanket in the back of the car if it is a hatchback. Otherwise put the puppy on the floor, between the rear seats, with a piece of blanket. Whenever you take a puppy, or an adult dog, out in the car, always carry a roll of paper towel. Accidents may happen and it is best to be prepared. Ensure that the doors are secure and the windows are open. The puppy can be taken with you when you go shopping, but not left for long periods of time, because boredom may set in and the car upholstery will get chewed. It is a good idea to have a soft toy in the car.

WORMING AND INOCULATIONS

First of all, the vet will examine the puppy carefully, checking the eyes and the ears and the condition of the coat. Oh yes! Some careless breeders sell puppies with fleas and skin conditions. If you have bought a dog puppy, the vet will check that he has two descended testicles. This is very important as you will have problems if one or both testicles fail to descend. The age at which this development takes place may vary from six to twelve weeks on average. After the external examination the vet will look at the mouth to check on the teeth, then take the temperature. If all is well, the puppy will be given the first part of the inoculations. Different vets have different systems and the inoculations may include extra drugs for treatment against kennel cough. Be sure you know what the inoculations are for. You should get a card carrying the date etc., so it can be used when you go for the first booster. The vet will ask you if the puppy has been wormed and what the outcome was. You will probably be given tablets, powder or liquid to worm the puppy at home. The tablets can be crushed and added to the food, or rolled in butter. If you have a syringe (without needle) you can put the syringe in the side of the mouth and press the plunger. Withdraw the syringe quickly, hold the muzzle tilted upwards and the puppy should swallow the liquid. Whatever the vet prescribes, you will find that administration depends on practice; practice makes perfect. At this point it is vital to remember that the vet is the best friend that your dog will have. Please do not just ring when you have an emergency and expect the vet to come running out. Regular visits will maintain a happy contact between vet and dog.

In the UK many owners take out an insurance policy for their dog, but this is not common practice in the US.

Chapter Four

TRAINING A BULLMASTIFF

HOUSE TRAINING

This begins as soon as you bring your puppy home. Usually the Bullmastiff is a very clean animal and seldom soils either bed or kennel. As I have said, your puppy must be put outside immediately upon wakening up and after finishing each meal. Please be patient and do not scold. Give praise when your puppy obliges. Every member of the household must follow the same routine, so that the puppy is not confused. "No" must mean "No". Always remember that a Bullmastiff puppy will grow into a big dog and, if not taught to obey you when young, will be pretty well uncontrollable when full grown.

Like small babies who are teething, puppies also like to bite something. Give them something hard to chew on, but make sure that it is not small enough to swallow, or brittle enough to break into small pieces which can also be swallowed. Avoid the use of shoes; don't be tempted to offer your old shoes. A shoe is a shoe to young puppies and it is difficult for them to understand why they have been scolded when they have ruined a pair of new shoes. Never allow a young puppy to have a friendly nibble of your hand. You must stamp out this habit from the outset. Habits formed in puppyhood are difficult to change. A friend used to allow his puppy to tug at his sleeve to draw attention. When cautioned about the stupidity of this action his reply was always the same: "The pup will grow out of it." Needless to say, many jacket sleeves were ruined in later years. If you do not intend your puppy to sleep on the settee or in the armchair, make this clear from the outset. After a few firm "No's" your Bullmastiff will realise that you mean business.

BASIC OBEDIENCE

Although we have domesticated dogs, they are basically wild animals. This can be seen in towns and cities where dogs are put out of doors without any thought about their welfare. They gather together and run around in packs with one dog as pack leader. In your home you must be the pack leader. This is essential with a breed which will grow to the size of a Bullmastiff. You must be firm but not harsh. The young puppy must learn to respect your wishes from the outset; but you must be consistent.

One of the first lessons is to get the puppy to sit. This is always a problem for a lively puppy, who wants to jump up. Gentle pressure on the rear end and the single word Sit, repeated at short intervals, should soon bring results. When you are satisfied, a few words of praise, Good boy or Good girl, or even a tidbit, will show your pleasure. The puppy, having learned to sit on command, can then be taught to stay behind. When the puppy is sitting, walking away for two or three yards for the first few attempts and, if the puppy tries to follow, lift up your hand, showing the dog your palm and give the command Stay. Push forward in the air with your hand so that the puppy can see

Ch. Dajean Red Dragon: Winner of 17 CCs, owned by G. Slater and Miss Jukes. The Bullmastiff is an intelligent breed and will respond well to training.

your intention. Extend this exercise until the puppy will stay quite a distance away from you. Once you are happy, remember to praise or reward the puppy.

The next step on basic Obedience is to get the puppy to come when called. Give the single word of command Come, after the puppy has been left for a short time in the Stay position. There we have three commands – Sit, Stay and Come – and the final one is Down. Most puppies try to jump up at some stage or other and this may spell danger for children or old people, if they are knocked over. A gentle push and the firm word Down is all that is needed. By nature, the Bullmastiff is not a noisy dog, seldom barking unless there is a reason for doing so. Sometimes a puppy may bark when excited. This must not be allowed to continue. A sharp No usually brings the barking to a halt.

OBEDIENCE TRAINING TARGETS

1 ATTENTIVENESS. If you always train your dog to watch you or your cues, it makes training so much easier to achieve good results. Cues, as with any training, are very important. As training becomes more advanced a lot of cues are eliminated, or abbreviated to such an extent that to a novice they are hard to spot. There are always some very obvious ones, such as stepping off with

Carrisme vom Dernbacher Reiter: The Bullmastiff will soon learn the basic Obedience exercises.

your left foot. This always means for your dog 'Heel work, let's go'. Whereas the right foot forward will be a cue for 'Stay work'. Advance work means there will not be a voice or hand signal, so your leg is a big cue for your dog, one always given. Your dog will also listen to the tone of your voice. "No" said in a gruff voice will probably stop the dog immediately, whereas a cheerful happy "Come" should have the dog bounding towards you as quickly as possible, just to be with you.

Body language is never mentioned but it is very important. Many people never fully realise its significance, especially with a work-out or trial. If you yourself are unsure, or doubt that your requests will be obeyed, then your dog probably will not do them. Body language is truly so important, so you have to watch your attitude more carefully than you think. The last cues are your hands. Again, most of these signals are eventually eliminated as the standard of training progresses. With Bullmastiffs, attentiveness is not always easy to attain. Early training demands a lot of work: quick turns; a click of the fingers; a tug of the lead; an occasional quick step. All these simple things will help to achieve results and to keep the dog's mind and body in tune with you.

2 WILLINGNESS. How receptive your dog is depends a lot on how willing he or she is to do your bidding and also, how consistent and persistent you are. Training has to be fun and if it is, the dog will be eager to try and please. This eagerness is a bonus; something to work on; and with it comes the little something that makes a house dog, or a competitive dog, a joy to live or work with. There are several ways to achieve this. Praise is always a good start. Food is another incentive, especially for a hungry Bullmastiff. Time out or Play is also a bonus and your dog will learn to love and look forward to these things. Combinations of these, can and do work successfully. Another item is simply to try to spend time watching your puppy or dog. Merely observing can reveal far more than you realise.

Flintstock Fine and Dandy (Joe), pictured with Toby, a five-year-old Pug. Joe has passed his Good Citizen test, and is now being trained in scent and retrieve. He is owned by Mr and Mrs Sanger, bred by Janet and Alex Gunn.

3 PACE. This can be achieved, but with Bullmastiffs it can be a big problem, as the breed is not a fast or flashy type of dog. They do things in their own time and this I have found is hard to change. Training time has to be short. That way you can pack a lot of pace into a short space of time and it seems to achieve best results. Working in small areas seems to work well. Attention should be more attuned to the Bullmastiff's forte for a slow pace. All of the Stay type of exercises create very little concern. I have also found that they can certainly Come when there is a biscuit at the end of it. Stay exercises seem to be the easiest part of the trials for this breed because they are so patient. The Bullmastiff was bred to be patient and silent, ready to pounce on an intruder. A game of Catch me seems to be a lot of fun and a surprising turn of speed and agility is there. Balls and sticks will help with a bit of fast work, as it keeps the pace going as well as the interest.

4 ACCURACY. Bullmastiffs have no problems doing things, but they are not always accurate. They will sit with their tails at an odd angle so they can be close to you. This is not difficult to adjust, but beware: Bullmastiffs are happy to be corrected time and time again if you are willing to

LEFT: Admiral von Hunnenstein and Aleyeska ex Britannia: The Bullmastiff can be surprisingly agile.

BELOW: Am. Ch. Watch Hill's Evita UD, Number One Obedience Bullmastiff in the US in 1986.   Photo: K. Booth.

Bulltzar Achilles CD retrieving a dumbbell. Anne Kenman trained Achilles and his sire to Companion Dog level.

do so. Be that as it may, they say that patience is a virtue, but in a trial ring sloppiness means points deducted. With this breed this can be ill-afforded. Most Judges are looking for accuracy with a fair pace. To some degree you have to adjust your pace to that of your dog; but a Bullmastiff will sometimes take advantage of the situation, if you are not aware of it.

Bullmastiffs learn quickly – a change of pace or a turn; a quick tap of the lead. A trick which my dogs learned early, was to sit straight. With this taught, a voice command would correct the crooked rear end and the dog would shuffle close to my side as if by magic. With the Drop, it is essential to watch hands and body, as there is a tendency to step too far forward to give the command. When taking part in trials you have a couple of steps in which you can adjust pace,

Fin. Ch. Renee drawing a sleigh: A well-trained Bullmastiff will take part in a variety of activities.

before you signal your dog. As training progresses, your dog learns to look for these clues. While the Sit creates few problems, the Drop creates more, especially with the Heel command likely to follow. A small step or two will be helpful to get a big dog moving again, so creating a smooth performance. When working your dog, try to fix your eyes on something so that you are working in a straight line. A check will get your dog into position, if out of line. The Come command should be so irresistible that it will propel your dog towards you. A happy voice and good body language also help. It is usual for Bullmastiffs to work at a fair pace – a steady trot – unlike a German Shepherd. Bullmastiffs learn quickly and once they know something they are unlikely to forget. They can be a little on the lazy side.

SOCIAL TRAINING
This is a facet of training that was unheard of in the past. An example of modern methods, now in use in many countries, is shown by Andrew Wilson BVMS, MRCVS, who has made it a great part of the work of the Orchard Veterinary Centre, in Nottingham, in the UK. A special invitation was sent out to a number of puppies.

Dear ....

We are holding a special party for puppies aged between 8 and 14 weeks on Wednesday July 12th from 7.30 to 8.30 pm. We should very much like you and your family to come. The party will last about 1 hour and there will be lots of things to do.
You will be greeted at the door by a vet, nurse or receptionist.
You can have a sniff around the consulting room, and a tour of the rest of the surgery without having anything done to you.
You can meet and play with all your fellow puppies, and one or two older dogs in the party room. There will be games to play.
There will be discussions on feeding, worming, house training, basic training, grooming, keeping

your teeth clean and lots more.

If you would like to come, please let us know during office hours by Monday July 10th. The first 10 puppies to reply can come! Space is limited.

We look forward to seeing you then!

Yours sincerely

PS Each puppy gets a small goody bag to go home with.

This party served a double purpose. Puppies were introduced to other puppies and dogs. They were also introduced to the idea of visiting the vets, which for some puppies is a frightening and painful ordeal. In many places, keen dog owners have started Puppy Classes. In the past there were Ringcraft Classes and Obedience Classes, but both were a little too advanced for young puppies. The sole object of a Puppy Class is socialisation. Puppies of all ages and sizes learn to play together. If you have not got such a class in your area, ask your vet to put an advertisement in the waiting room, inviting puppy owners to meet together to form such a class.

PROBLEM BEHAVIOUR

With careful training from a very early age, problem behaviour should not develop. Although it is not advisable to allow any Tom, Dick or Harry to walk in and handle young puppies, contact must be made with people at an early age, say at about five or six weeks. This is especially good for people who are purchasing a new puppy. If possible there should be two or three meetings before the puppy goes to the new home. In this way the new owners become familiar – they are not strangers. Puppies reared in kennels, and with little human contact, are often timid when they meet other people, and dogs, for the first time. This fear of people may, in some cases, turn to aggression. Meal times can create problems with greedy puppies and dogs. Each must have a dish and no dog must be allowed to take another dog's food. It is easier to put all the food on one big dish, but the 'poor-doer' does not get a fair ration.

Some dogs become 'problem dogs' as the result of bad training in the home. Owners must learn to recognise the difference between possessiveness and protectiveness. Some owners find it almost impossible to take objects away from their dogs. This is stupid. If a dog has picked up a dangerous object, or a forbidden object, a sharp command from the owner "Drop it", should be sufficient for the dog to drop the offending article. It was always a source of amazement when a one-time next-door neighbour of ours, who owned a Yorkshire Terrier, said she could not take anything away from her dog. "How is it, you can take those huge marrow bones away from your big dogs and I cannot take anything away from my little one?" she would ask.

If a dog is allowed to become over-protective of an owner, this could lead to problems if the owner is taken ill. Also remember this: if there are young children in the household you must instil in them the basic knowledge that no dog, not even a Bullmastiff, can stand screaming. A dog's hearing is so acute that a high-pitched scream will arouse them from a deep sleep.

Children must also learn that a dog does not always want to play. Sometimes a child will call a puppy who is eating, or is resting. A well-trained puppy, or an adult dog, will growl, which is the canine equivalent of saying "I don't want to play". A sensible child will heed the dog's warning. A child who does not do this may get bitten and, believe me, a bite from a Bullmastiff can be a big bite. You must reason with the child, and ask what he or she would do if someone still wanted to play if they had said they didn't want to play any more. The usual answer is either, "I would give him a big push" or, "I would kick him". Ask the child: "Have you ever seen a dog push anyone?"

or "Have you seen a dog kick anyone?" No! A dog cannot push and a dog cannot kick. Then you can say: "A dog who growls is asking to be left alone. If you refuse to listen, all a dog can do is to use the only weapon they have – their teeth."

If an otherwise placid dog begins to show signs of aggression, check the ears to see if there is any sign of infection. Check other parts of the body to see if there are any swellings or sore places. You know yourself that if anyone touches a sore spot on you, your first impulse is to raise your hand and ward off the offender. A dog may growl, or snap. Look out for this sign; do not ignore it. One important fact to remember: if you have a dog with temperament problems, do not try to place the dog in another home or put it in Rescue. If you have sought advice from the vet, act on that advice. If the vet suggests euthanasia, face up to it. Put the dog to sleep with dignity and live with your conscience. On the whole, bitches seem to have fewer behavioural problems than dogs, but when bitches fight, they can be as vicious as any dog. If two bitches are kept together they can be 'touchy' when one or the other comes into season. It is not unusual for one to 'mount' the other, like a dog. Our first two bitches did this. However, after one bitch had been mated and produced a litter, she did not like her sister's advances. From then on, they were segregated during their seasons.

The question which new owners often ask is: "When do we teach the dog to guard?" The simple answer is: "You don't teach Bullmastiffs to guard. It is a natural instinct. It is enough that they look as if they are a guard dog." If you have more than one Bullmastiff, always be prepared for trouble, though it may never happen. If you keep them in pairs, always have a bucket of water, or an old coat or blanket at the ready. At the first sign of aggression, the water thrown over the heads acts as a short, sharp shock. The coat or blanket, when thrown over the heads, obscures the light and confuses the dogs. Separate the offending animals as quickly as possible.

Never try to force a dog to look at you with full 'eye to eye' contact. Few, if any dogs will accept this, and will see it as a challenge to fight. You can look your dog in the eye when you are giving praise, but do not be surprised if the dog turns away and looks over your shoulder. Never tease so much that a dog becomes over-tired, or over-excited. If you can see the eyes becoming bright with excitement, stop the teasing or the game. You, and members of your family, must always be in complete control. You are the pack leaders. If the dog does not obey, you must not administer a thrashing, as this may cause the dog to bite in self-defence. Speak in a harsh voice and put the offender away for a period of time. The tone of voice and the exclusion from all the usual places, should be sufficient to show the dog that wrong has been done, and you are not pleased.

TRAINING FOR THE SHOW RING

Assuming that your Bullmastiff is a puppy, training can begin as soon as the settling-in period is over. As with Obedience training, a Bullmastiff soon gets bored, so two short periods daily are much better than one long period. The puppy will already be used to a collar and lead. There are various types of collars: flat leather, fastening with a buckle; rolled leather working on the same principle as a choke chain; and a metal choke chain. If you use either of the last two, ensure that it is put on correctly. When tension is applied to the lead, it tightens across the top of the neck first. As the tension is released, the collar or choker loosens, because the bulk of the collar is under the neck. If in doubt, ask the other exhibitors, your vet, or your puppy's breeder.

Teach your puppy to run in a straight line from the outset. Find the pace best suited to your puppy. If the puppy begins to gallop (both hind legs moving together in unison), the pace is too fast; if the puppy paces (both legs on the one side moving in unison), the pace is too slow. A sharp tug on the lead will be sufficient to change pace. The lead should be long enough to pass across the front of the exhibitor's body; the loop or handle, should be held firmly in the right hand. The

*Training for the
show ring should
begin at an early
age.*

*Am. Can. Mex. Int.
Ch. Little Caesar
ROM, owned by
Dean and Claudette
Aamodt, winner of
more than 250 Best
of Breed wins,
numerous group
placements, and two
regional Specialty
wins.
The combination of
a well-trained dog
and a skilful
handler is a great
bonus in the show
ring.*

left hand should rest lightly on the lead so that it can be used to give a sharp tug towards the body.

When you progress to moving the puppy in a triangle, a slight tug with the left hand will bring the puppy over, without upsetting the rhythm. Two hands are essential if you want to have full control. Keep the puppy on your left hand side so that, when you move from right to left, across the top of the triangle, the judge or trainer has an unobstructed view. When the judge or trainer asks you to move your puppy in a straight line, remember that a straight line is the shortest distance between two points. When you get to the furthest point, a sharp tug will bring the puppy towards you and you can move smartly around the outside of the puppy without upsetting the rhythm. If you have a good friend or neighbour, they can help by going over your puppy. Some puppies respond magnificently when the owner says "Teeth". If it is a poor mouth they usually allow judge or trainer to have a good look at their teeth; if it is a good mouth they almost always clench their teeth tightly. If the puppy can be examined daily, so much the better. It becomes a habit.

Once you feel that you and your puppy are moving together as a pair, try to find a ring training class in your area. Be sure the training is for the ring and not Obedience, as the basic training is very different. The class will usually cater for dogs of various breeds and ages. This will provide good social training, as well as training the puppy for entry in Variety Classes. From time to time ring training classes will have special nights when there is an award for the best handler and dog. Remember that it is a ring training class and the prize is being awarded for the rapport between you and your dog. The trainer may not know the virtues or the faults in your dog, but will know whether or not you show your dog well.

If you have enjoyed the camaraderie of the ring training class and now you feel you would like to go further, find out where the nearest breed club is and apply for membership. Most breed clubs have handbooks, newsletters etc. and you will find these invaluable. All hold shows at different times of the year. If you can, get along to a few of these shows, preferably without your dog. Watch how the exhibitors handle their dogs and ask questions. Look and listen. This way you will learn how to show your dog to advantage. A good dog can lose a first prize because of bad handling, and can be beaten by an inferior dog which is well handled. Remember always that the Bullmastiff is a unique breed. You must not try to gait one like a German Shepherd Dog; nor must you extend a Bullmastiff's hindquarters like a Boxer. The Bullmastiff is a powerful dog, strong but not cumbersome, sound and active. Standing, a good Bullmastiff is a magnificent animal – not too big, not too small. Moving, the dog shows strength and power. A Bullmastiff is a natural breed; the coat is not trimmed or clipped; the tail is not docked. If a puppy has straight stifles or a high back end, stretching out the hind legs will not fool a good judge. The same applies to movement; moving too quickly will not disguise bad movement.

Chapter Five

CARE OF THE BULLMASTIFF

Unfortunately the Bullmastiff is not known for having a long life span, but with tender loving care there is no reason why the normal dog should not live to be eleven or twelve years of age. Housing is most important. After always living indoors, a Bullmastiff should not be pushed outdoors when the dog is no longer used at stud or, in the case of a bitch, she is no longer producing puppies.

LIVING INDOORS

We have always used the large plastic beds with a double layer of one of the hygienic types of dog bedding. The beds can be placed where there is no danger of a draught. The bedding must be washed regularly and the bed itself can be scrubbed out with soap, water and a good disinfectant. Internally, the largest size bed is approximately 33 inches or 84 centimetres across by 23 inches or 58 centimetres in depth. The sloping sides are approximately 8 inches or 20 centimetres deep and the front opening is 15 inches or 38 centimetres wide. As the bed is oval in shape the dog curls up quite comfortably. There are metal beds with canvas covering the base and the sides, but we found that these tended to sag in the middle. There are huge bean bags which appeal to some dogs, but from time to time the beans must be replaced as they tend to disintegrate.

Aust. Ch. Nightwatch Sweet Embrace, owned by the Bullmaster kennel.
The Bullmastiff, with its short coat, is a low maintenance breed as far as grooming is concerned.
Photo: Animal Pics.

LIVING OUTDOORS

If the dog is to be housed outdoors, the first priority is to ensure that the kennel is weatherproof and well insulated. A stable-type door, with the top and bottom halves opening separately, affords easy access for cleaning and the top half can be closed during cooler weather. A short inner panel or wall, near the door opening, will protect the dog from draughts. A sash, or hopper window, will allow light and extra ventilation. If heating is used during cold weather, ensure that it is properly installed. Avoid the use of oil heaters as these can be knocked over. Sometimes an elderly dog may become a little deaf, so a smoke alarm would not come amiss. The bed may be of the type used indoors. Alternatively wood-wool, straw or blankets may be used. The first two must be changed regularly and the third washed regularly. The walls and the floor must be cleaned at least twice every week. The outer run, or compound, must be cleaned daily, as stale faeces or urine are a magnet for flies and disease.

DIET

Unless an adult dog is obese or ill, the diet need not provide any problems. If your dog is used to a complete diet, continue with this, but divide it into two or three small meals. Cut down on tidbits and fattening foods. Give the last small meal two or three hours before you go to bed and remove all uneaten food before you retire. The ideal for the older adult dogs is to keep them light in weight, as they are no longer growing and, quite often, they do not get as much exercise. This is why the meals are spread into small amounts and the daily intake can be less. Far more health problems are caused by overfeeding than underfeeding. Complete diets are, as the name implies, complete. Statisticians, dieticians and veterinary surgeons are employed to work together to produce a diet which contains all the essentials for building body and bone, plus a healthy digestive system etc. It is not only unnecessary, but it is highly dangerous to give supplements with any complete meal. If you have any problems consult your vet or, better still, the makers of the food.

We have been lucky because we have been able to rear and maintain our Bullmastiffs on natural foods, such as ox tripe, liver, heart, and fish, plus cheese with the occasional boiled or fried egg. The supplement was sterilised bone meal. Ox tripe can be cut into small pieces and deep frozen. Liver, heart and fish must be cooked, and the latter carefully checked for bones. For an occasional treat, a tin of sardines provides a tasty variation. Never mix raw and cooked foods together. A small amount of mixer meal may be mixed with tinned food. Thick wholemeal bread, baked in a slow oven is also useful and popular. Feed your dog as well as you can, but always remember, a little good food is far better than a lot of bulk food. A bowl of clean drinking water must always be available. If you can buy a large marrow bone from time to time, it will give your dog a lot of pleasure and it will exercise the jaw muscles. Once your dog has stripped off all the remnants of meat, saw the bone across to expose the marrow. Dogs love this – it is a great delicacy. A long fork or spoon will enable you to clean the bone out. Avoid small bones which are found in poultry, rabbit or fish. If you soak food with gravy, check that all bones are removed. Small bones can lodge in the back teeth. If your dog begins to dribble, or to paw the sides of the jaw, check the teeth for fragments of bone or other hard material. Small bones can also stick in the throat, causing distress, or may pass into the stomach. If this happens the outcome is often fatal.

EXERCISE

A dog aged eighteen months or more can be given plenty of exercise. If you can, vary the type of ground from time to time. Hard ground will help to keep the toe nails short, while softer, firmer ground will help to tighten the feet. Moving up and down on a steep slope or hill-side will help strengthen the shoulder muscles and the second thighs. When I am asked how much exercise mature Bullmastiffs need, my reply is always the same: "They need as much or as little as you are willing to give." Kelly, our original Bullmastiff, used a game of 'tug of war' to strengthen her shoulder muscles. If she had a bath, it was almost impossible to rub her down with the towel as she insisted on tugging at the end of it. If you released the towel, the game ceased. Her favourite exercise was leaping and bounding in very long grass. Even the 'Senior Citizens' appreciate a little gentle exercise. A gentle stroll, two or three times a day is all they ask. If it rains, make sure that you rub their coats dry.

Della and Donn of Kelwall playing in the snow. Bullmastiffs enjoy the stimulation of exercise, and this includes playing with other dogs.

GROOMING

We look at the coat first. A daily brushing works wonders. I use the word 'brushing' loosely. What you use depends on you and your dog. We have used gloves, chamois leathers and bristle brushes but, for the last few years, we have used contraptions made up of various types of rubber bristles. They do not damage the skin but they do bring out any loose hairs. On average, the Bullmastiff moults twice per year, in the spring and the autumn. There may be a slight change in colour – lighter in spring and darker in autumn. Because of the type of coat, there is very little loose hair. With a dog who is in good condition, who is groomed daily, and has good clean sleeping quarters, there is no call for regular bathing. Constant bathing spoils the texture of the coat. A shower of rain or a dip in the sea will keep your dog smelling sweet. There should be no doggy smell with a healthy Bullmastiff. From experience, I can assure you that the dog will not have an unpleasant smell. A dog who has been out in the rain should have all the mud wiped off, particularly on the underside, and the back rubbed dry with a coarse towel. If your dog rolls in mud or offensive-smelling material then you will have to resort to a bath. If this has to be carried out indoors, you will need help. If conditions are suitable, you can do the task outdoors with the aid of a length of hose attached to the kitchen or bathroom taps. With a good canine shampoo, and water that is neither too hot nor too cold, plus a thick, rough towel, it is easy. Rinse the coat well, and be extremely careful the shampoo and the water do not get into the eyes or the ears. Most dogs usually shake themselves vigorously, so stand well back. Finish off with a brisk rub with the towel.

When you groom the dog, look for evidence of fleas or ticks. Fleas can be brought in by cats, or they may be from hedgehogs in the garden. Ticks usually abound in areas where there are sheep and, sometimes, hedgehogs. Because of the short, close-lying coat, many of us do not see these parasites on our dogs. Flea excrement resembles minute fragments of black grit amongst the dog's hair. Ticks are small grey objects which cling to the dog's skin and are very difficult to remove. There are many remedies on sale for the clearance of fleas. If the infestation is heavy, the whole house or kennel may have to be treated. Ticks can be removed by applying a pad of cotton wool soaked in surgical spirit, dry-cleaning fluid or nail-varnish remover to them. When the tick has been soaked, it will come away. Do not attempt to remove them forcibly, as you may not extract the mouth parts; if left behind they can cause infection. As always, if in doubt, consult your vet.

Next we look at the nails. If a dog has good, tight, cat feet the nails will be short. If the feet are splayed, you may have to clip the nails. With some dogs this is easier said than done, and you may have to go along to your vet. There are various types of nail clippers on the market and some of them are quite expensive. Ask a friend for the loan of theirs before you buy any. If your dog allows you to cut the nails, take great care not to cut them too short. If you make them bleed the chances are your dog will never allow you to cut them again. Believe me, Bullmastiffs saying "No" to a manicure/pedicure, really mean it. They lie on their back and all four legs kick out in all directions – and a Bullmastiff can kick!

Next on the list comes teeth. A dog who, as a puppy, has got used to a regular teeth examination will also have got used to having them cleaned. Nowadays, there are flavoured toothpastes which can be used to advantage. There are also many types of dog chews which help strengthen the jaw as well as cleaning the teeth. If you use a dog chew ensure that it is not too small, because if it is, there would be the danger that the dog could swallow it whole. If in doubt, watch the dog carefully and remove any unsuitable chews. Good big biscuits are also useful. If the teeth develop signs of tartar consult your vet. The teeth can then be cleaned under general anaesthetic.

Ears must be examined daily. The ear folds can be cleansed gently with good-quality cotton wool (cotton), cotton buds or cleansing tissues. Never probe deeply into the ear canal. If there is any kind of discharge or a strange smell, consult your vet immediately. From time to time grass seeds can work their way into the inner ear, necessitating surgery. If your dog shows signs of discomfort, such as violent head-shaking or scratching, examine the ears gently and carefully. If in doubt make an appointment with your vet. A single bottle of prescription ear-drops can clear up many problems quickly and easily. Neglect may cause unnecessary suffering and, in some cases, may even lead to severe temperament problems. It is always better to be safe than sorry.

INFECTIOUS AND CONTAGIOUS DISEASES

It is of importance to note that some diseases contracted by the dog can be passed on to the humans. Therefore it cannot be stressed too often than cleanliness is essential. Kennels, beds, blankets, food and water bowls must all be kept scrupulously clean. Do not leave stale food lying around where it can be contaminated by flies and other creatures. There are many causes of infectious diseases and, as a layman, I can only offer a basic guide. As with humans, some dogs are more susceptible to infection than others; some have an acquired resistance or immunity; some are carriers. An infectious disease must not be confused with a contagious disease. An infectious disease can result from an infected bite from a flea, a wasp or another dog. The bite or puncture becomes infected. A contagious disease is caused by direct or indirect contact. All contagious disease are infectious, but not all infectious diseases are contagious.

If a newborn puppy does not receive colostrum suckled from the mother soon after birth (should, for example, the bitch not have any milk) the vet may inject a dose of Antisera, which is rather like

UK and Am. Ch. Cadenham Blonde Ambition. Regular, routine health checks, supervised exercise and a top-quality diet with lead to a happy, fit dog.

Photo: Martin Leigh.

a substitute. In puppies the immune systems develop while they are still in the womb, during the second half of pregnancy. By four weeks of age, the puppies will have developed an immune system capable of responding to infections. Some animals become immune to infection by being exposed to it, and puppies can be immunised or vaccinated to prevent infection. This immunity may last for a lifetime or a few months. In a few cases, puppies which are in poor condition due to bad rearing, illness or starvation, may have a deficiency in their immune system, which will then not function as it should. If you have a large number of dogs, it is wise to have a separate kennel in which you can isolate dogs which develop an infectious disease. Even if you have only got one or two dogs, you must keep any new dogs or puppies away from infected dogs for at least two or three weeks. As soon as possible you must get your puppy vaccinated, and you must keep up with the boosters every year. The type of vaccination rests with your vet. Under normal circumstances the puppy will be vaccinated against distemper (hard pad), infectious canine hepatitis, leptospirosis and parvovirus. Following primary vaccination the puppy should not be exposed to infection for at least seven days. A small number of puppies may fail to respond to vaccination. If there are any adverse reactions, consult your vet immediately.

CANINE DISTEMPER is one of the oldest and best-known diseases of the dog. In slight cases there may be decreased appetite, a fever, and a slight discharge from the eyes and nose. There may even be a slight cough. If in doubt, isolate the dog. In severe cases it may start out as above, but the discharge from the nose gets thicker and the eyes redden. The cough is much worse. The dog may develop 'fits' – the eyes twitch, and the dog champs its jaws and begins to dribble. The pads are thickened and hard, developing deep cracks – hard pad. Seek advice immediately and isolate the patient.

INFECTIOUS CANINE HEPATITIS can be very painful. The dog is very ill and may develop a temperature of up to 106°F. The lymph nodes and tonsils are swollen and if you touch the ribs, the dog may groan in pain. The dog is usually very thirsty, vomits frequently and may pass blood-tinged diarrhoea. The linings of the mouth and eyes may be pale, due to lack of blood. The pulse is rapid and breathing is often fast and shallow. Sad to say, most dogs which develop signs of ICH will die.

LEPTOSPIROSIS The first signs are usually dullness, fever and loss of appetite. The most severe cases often collapse and die without showing any more distinctive signs than those. In less severe cases, the dog vomits and blood may be seen. There may be scanty, black diarrhoea. The dog may moan in distress, with liver swelling causing pain in the abdomen to such an extent that the dog resents being handled. Severe shock and dehydration are likely to result in death. In the other type of leptospirosis the onset is usually shown by dullness, loss of appetite and high temperature. Ten or more days later the dog may show signs of kidney failure and, in severe cases, no urine at all is passed. The dog's back arches because of the pain. The dog may vomit more frequently as the kidney failure develops and may show signs of ulcers in the mouth. The breath may begin to smell of ammonia and the dog becomes dehydrated and collapses. Special mention must be made here that *Leptospirosis is a serious and sometimes fatal disease in humans*. Care and absolute cleanliness is essential and advice must be sought if you have the slightest inkling that you have an infected dog.

PARVOVIRUS shows a wide variation in course and severity. A puppy suffering from parvovirus enteritis may be listless on the first day, vomiting on the second day, and the third day will collapse, with bloody diarrhoea. The diarrhoea smells foul. Some puppies may die within twenty-four hours, due to dehydration. Dehydration shows when you pull the skin into a peak over the shoulders and it is very slow to return to its normal position. The first indication of parvovirus myocarditis is the sudden death of puppies of three to four weeks of age. They appear healthy but they may drop dead while they are feeding or playing. Some may survive for six to eight weeks, but they fail to grow properly; they have difficulty breathing and the abdomen may swell. If any of the puppies in a litter is confirmed to be a victim of parvovirus myocarditis, all the litter-mates are likely to be affected. They may survive for some time, but may die of heart failure when quite young. None of the puppies in a litter so affected must be sold as normal puppies. Adults and weaned puppies with parvovirus enteritis do not develop heart problems.

KENNEL COUGH is characterised by coughing and is most common in dogs which are in, or have been, in kennels. It can be transmitted in any place where a lot of dogs are gathered together – this means training classes and dog shows, for example. The actual cough may be harsh and dry, or moist. It may last for a few days, or three weeks or more. It may cause the dog to vomit. In the early days the dog may sneeze, thus spreading the infection. In many cases the dog has bright eyes and does not lose its appetite. Dogs and puppies which are in a poor condition may develop pneumonia. Isolate any suspect as soon as possible and *do not take any contacts to a show or training class.* One infected dog can pass the infection to many more in the space of one day. Prevention is better than cure. Keep your kennels clean and dry. Have a good supply of disinfectant on hand. If needs be, do not be afraid to get down on your knees to scrub the floor. Invest in a good thermometer.

SKIN DISEASES: A very young puppy may develop impetigo (puppy pyoderma). There are many small pustules (pimples) on the non-hairy skin – round the lips and on the belly. It can be caused by a dirty environment, poor nutrition or infection by parasites. Slight cases may heal without treatment but in severe cases you may have to use a medicated shampoo.
Acute Moist Dermatitis: This often appears in summer when the atmosphere is humid. It may be due to flea allergy or anal sac disease. It is very painful and many animals will not allow you to touch the infected area. Veterinary advice and treatment is essential. The vet will clip the infected area and wash it with a medicated shampoo. There may be a need for ointment and some oral medication.
Deep Folliculitis: This involves the roots of the hair (follicles). It may be possible to see brown or reddish crusts on the surface, or there may be openings in the skin which ooze pus, if gently pressed. Isolate the dog and seek advice. If neglected, it may take a long time for the skin to heal.
Canine acne: This is a chronic disease affecting the lips and chin of young, short-coated dogs. If affects the deep parts of the hair follicles and the surrounding skin. It is not always easy to see, as it does not seem to upset the dog in any way. The affected places may heal without treatment, but if it is still apparent when the dog is twelve months old or more, seek veterinary advice. There are many skin problems brought about by fleas, ticks, harvest mites etc. Some dogs are also allergic to the synthetic fibres which are used in the manufacture of modern household carpets. The cleaning powders and sprays which are used around the house can also affect the skin of some dogs. If your dog is continually scratching, make a careful examination to see if there is an infestation. If the scratching continues, seek advice.

EARS: The ear flaps must be kept clean. Baby wipes or clean gauze are excellent for this task. Do not allow any moisture to fall inside the ear. From time to time there may be a dark, waxy secretion inside the ear canal. The vet will provide a course of drops which should clear the condition. If the secretion continues, the vet may advise surgery for the removal of a foreign body, such as grass seed, and will provide a large plastic collar which will stop the dog from scratching until the incision has healed.

EYES: The main problem affecting the eyes of a Bullmastiff is entropion. It has been said that a good vet can 'correct' the condition and no one will know that it was there. This is good for the well-being of the animal concerned, but the animal should not be used in any breeding programme. In the US it would be illegal to show the dog after such surgery. The consensus of opinion points to the condition being hereditary, although in rare cases it can be brought about by injury or malnutrition. The dog blinks and avoids the sun and bright lights. There is excessive 'weeping'. The condition, when not brought on by an injury, usually shows up in the first six months of life. It can be seen that the eyelids are turning in on the eyeball and, as the eyelids move, the eyelashes damage the eyeball. This can cause ulcers and, if neglected, can cause blindness in the affected eye. The condition is due to an excess of eyelid, or a small eye, or both. If you intend to pursue a breeding programme, these are two points to look for in any dog which you may consider. If you suspect entropion, do not hesitate to seek advice, because it is very painful for your dog, apart from the fact that it may result in the loss of sight.

THE LOCOMOTOR SYSTEM: Although there are now so many balanced foods and complete diets on the market, there would appear to be an increase in the problems involving movement. **Hip dysplasia:** This is a problem that particularly affects the Bullmastiff. What causes HD? If only there was an answer which would satisfy everyone! It is hereditary, according to some sources, and environmental, according to others. Others will say it is brought on by trauma or over-exercise in puppyhood. The age at which it becomes apparent is variable. A young puppy may be reluctant to walk or play and may have difficulty getting up from a lying position. As the puppy grows, the weight is thrown forward onto the shoulders, to relieve the strain on the hips. The hindquarters begin to lack muscle tone (no well-developed second thigh) and the shoulders are overloaded. In later years the affected puppy will probably suffer from arthritis. There is no remedy for this condition, but the vet can prescribe pain-killers. In some countries there is a strict control on the breeding programme of Bullmastiffs. They must be X-rayed before breeding can take place and two highly-scored animals will not be allowed to breed together.

Osteochondrosis: This is becoming a talking point in many circles, although it was unheard of in Bullmastiffs a few years ago. It affects the cartilage of the joints and it may slow down the growth of bone. The limbs may become distorted. I cannot help feeling that some exhibitors are trying to "mature" their dogs far too early. They are giving extra vitamins and calcium in an attempt to give the good bone which is necessary in an adult dog. Too much of a vitamin is just as bad as too little. Our breed is renowned as a slow developer, reaching maturity at two and a half to three years of age. It is rare for a dog under two years of age to become a Champion.

Rupture of the Cruciate Ligaments: More and more Bullmastiffs are receiving surgery for ruptured cruciate ligaments in the stifle joints. This injury is common in many old, overweight or large dogs. Sometimes the first sign of injury is sudden. The dog may be running around and a sudden, swift change of direction may cause the dog to yelp in pain. A long period of rest may ease the situation. In other dogs there may be intermittent signs of lameness which gradually get worse. The stifle joint may be slightly swollen but not very painful and the dog may flex the injured limb to the extent that just the toes are touching the ground. If you have any doubts, consult your vet immediately. In slight cases pain killers and rest may suffice. If the injury is serious, the vet may advise surgery to repair the ruptured ligament. There are many different methods used, and the one chosen depends on your vet. Follow all instructions to the letter regarding rest and exercise when you bring the dog home. Care taken at this stage may help control the incidence of osteo-arthritis at a later date.

BONE TUMOURS: These are generally malignant, so any treatment, including amputation, does not provide a cure.

LEUKAEMIA AND LYMPHOSARCOMA: The former is a disease of the white blood cells. Lymphosarcoma affects many parts of the body – the lymph nodes begin to swell. Both of these conditions are difficult for the layman to diagnose. In leukaemia the dog may become listless and refuse food. The lips and inner eyelids become very pale due to anaemia. Research is still being carried out on these conditions, especially in the Bullmastiff.

I do not profess to be a veterinarian or a veterinary surgeon. I have simply tried to highlight the problems which do affect Bullmastiffs. Some can be avoided if care is taken about hygiene and correct feeding, especially with young puppies. Allow the puppy to develop naturally. *Do not over-feed. Do not over-exercise.* Avoid the use of supplements, especially if you are feeding a complete, balanced meal.

Chapter Six

THE BREED STANDARDS

STANDARD OF POINTS

A notice in the UK *Kennel Gazette* for October 1925 stated: "The Secretary reported having received a letter from the Midland Bull Mastiff Club asking the Committee to accept a Standard of Points for Bull Mastiffs, to which he had pointed out that the Kennel Club does not lay down or publish a Standard of points in any breed. The Committee confirmed the reply of the Secretary."

STANDARD TYPE OF BULL-MASTIFF (BRITISH) 1926

The National Bull-Mastiff Police Dog Club was granted permission to register its title in February 1926. A card containing rules and 'Standard Type of Bull-Mastiff' was issued to members with the proviso that the Standard was 'drawn up by Mr S. E. Moseley and accepted by the Club'.

In general appearance the Bull-Mastiff is a noble symmetrical animal with well-knit frame, powerful but active, courageous but docile. Dogs should be 26 to 28 inches at the shoulder and 90 to 110 lbs in weight. Bitches 25 to 27 inches and 80 to 90 lbs.

The head should be large and square with fair wrinkle. Muzzle not more than 3 inches long, deep

Ch. Tiger Prince: The breed's first dog Champion, 1928.

and broad. Nostrils large and broad. Flews not too pendulous, stop moderate, mouth level favouring projection of the lower rather than the upper incisors. Canine teeth large and set wide. Eyes dark and of medium size, set apart the width of muzzle with furrow between. Dark mask preferable. Skull large and may measure almost equal the height of the dog, it should be broad, with cheeks well developed. Forehead flat, ears V or folded back, set on wide and high, level with occiput and cheek, giving a square appearance to the skull. Neck slightly arched, moderate length, very muscular and almost equal in circumference to skull. Chest wide and deep, well set down between forelegs. Girth may be up to a third more than the dog's height. Ribs arched, deep and well set back to hips. Back short, giving a compact carriage. Shoulders muscular and slightly sloping. Arms powerful, elbows square, forelegs straight well boned and set wide apart. Pasterns straight, feet large with round toes, well arched. Loins wide and muscular slightly arched with fair depth of flank. Hind legs broad and muscular with well developed second thigh denoting power but not cumbersome. Hocks slightly bent, "cow hocks" or "splay feet" are most undesirable. Tail set high up, strong at the root and tapering, reaching to or just below the hocks, straight or curved but never carried gay or hound fashion. Coat short and dense giving good weather protection. Colour, any shade of fawn or brindle.

POINTS

Symmetry and general character	10
Body height and substance	10
Skull	10
Foreface and muzzle	15
Ears	5
Eyes	5
Chest and ribs	10
Forelegs and feet	10
Back loins and flank	10
Hindquarters, legs and feet and tail	10
Coat and colour	5
Total	**100**

STANDARD OF TYPE OF THE BULLMASTIFF (BRITISH) 1943
In 1943, the Southern Bullmastiff Society and Training Club revised the Standard and scale of points, bringing both up to date.
No 1 General Impression The Bullmastiff is a powerfully built dog, symmetrical, and showing great strength, but not cumbersome. Of a refined type, not to be confused with either the Bulldog or the Mastiff. His temperament combines high spirits, reliability, activity, endurance and alertness. **15**
No 2 Size and Weight Dogs should be 25 ins. to 27 ins. at the shoulder, and 100 lb. to 125 lb. in weight. Bitches should be 24 ins. to 26 ins. at the shoulder, and 90 lb. to 110 lb. in weight. It must be borne in mind that size must be proportionate with weight, and soundness and activity is most essential. **5**
No 3 The Skull This should be large and square viewed from every angle, with fair wrinkle when interested, but not when in repose. The skull may measure the height of the dog; it should be broad and deep with good cheeks. **6**

No 4 The Muzzle Short, broad under the eyes, not more than three and a half inches long and keeping nearly parallel in width to the end of the nose; blunt and cut off square, this forming a right angle with the upper line of the face, and at the same time proportionate with the skull. Under jaw broad to the end. **Nose** broad with widely spreading nostrils when viewed from the front; flat, not pointed or turned up in profile. **Flews** not pendulous, and not to hang below the level of the bottom of the lower jaw. **Stop** definite. **10**

No 5 Mouth and Teeth Mouth to be level, slight undershot allowed, but not preferred. Canine teeth large and set wide apart, other teeth strong, even and well spaced. Irregularity of teeth a definite fault. **3**

No 6 Eyes Dark or hazel, and of medium size, set apart the width of the muzzle, with furrow between. Light or yellow eyes a definite fault. **3**

No 7 Ears "V" shaped, or folded back, set on wide and high, level with occiput, giving a square appearance to the skull, which is most important. They should be small and denser in colour than the body, and the point of the ear should be level with the eyes when alert. Rose ears to be penalised. **3**

No 8 Neck Well-arched, moderate length, very muscular and almost equal to the skull in circumference. **3**

No 9 Chest Wide and deep, well set down between forelegs, with deep brisket. **6**

No 10 Girth and Ribs The girth may be up to one third more than the height of the dog. **Ribs** well sprung, deep and well set back to the hips, giving a rounded appearance. **3**

No 11 Shoulders Muscular and powerful, not overloaded. **3**

No 12 Back Short and straight, giving a compact carriage, but not so short as to interfere with activity. Roach and sway backs a fault. **6**

No 13 Loins Wide and muscular with fair depth of flank. **3**

No 14 Arms Powerful forelegs, straight, well boned and set wide apart, presenting a straight front. **3**

No 15 Pasterns Straight and strong. **2**

No 16 Feet Not large, with rounded toes, well arched (cat feet), pads hard, splay feet a decided fault. **3**

No 17 Hind Legs Strong and muscular, with well-developed second thighs, denoting power and activity, but not cumbersome. **6**

No 18 Hocks Moderately bent. Cows hocks a decided fault. **3**

No 19 Tail Set high, strong at root and tapering, reaching to the hocks, carried straight or curved, but not hound fashion. Crank tails a fault. **3**

No 20 Coat Short and hard, giving weather protection, lying flat to the body. A tendency to silky or woolly coats to be penalised. Long coats not eligible for competition. **6**

No 21 Colour Any shade of brindle, fawn or red, but either colour to be pure and clear. A slight white marking on chest permissible, but not desirable. Other white markings a definite fault. A black muzzle is essential, toning off towards the eyes, with dark markings around the eyes, giving expression. **5**

THE BRITISH BULLMASTIFF LEAGUE JANUARY 1956
This was the year when the Standard was lined up in the way which we have come to accept. The scale of points was abandoned.

STANDARD OF TYPE
General Appearance The Bullmastiff is a powerfully built dog, and showing great strength but

*Ch. Ambassador of
Buttonoak, bred by Mr and
Mrs E.L. Terry in 1953,
and used as a role model
for the breed.*

not cumbersome. His temperament combines high spirits, reliability, activity, endurance and alertness.

Head and Skull The skull should be large and square, viewed from every angle, with fair wrinkle. The skull may measure the height of the dog, it should be broad and deep, with good cheeks. The muzzle short, broad under the eyes, not more than three and a half inches long, and keeping parallel in width at the end of the nose, blunt and cut off square, this forming a right angle with the upper line of the face, and at the same time proportionate with the skull. Under jaw broad to the end. Nose broad with widely spreading nostrils when viewed from the front; flat, not pointed or turned up in profile. Flews not pendulous and not to hang below the level of the bottom of the lower jaw.

Stop Definite.

Eyes Dark or hazel and of medium size, set apart the width of the muzzle, with furrow between. Light or yellow eyes a definite fault.

Ears V shaped or folded back, set on wide and high, level with occiput, giving a square appearance to the skull which is most important. They should be small and deeper in colour than the body, and the point of the ear should be level with the eye when alert. Rose ears to be penalised.

Mouth Mouth to be level, slight undershot allowed but not preferred; canine teeth large and set wide apart; other teeth strong, even and well placed. Irregularity of teeth a definite fault.

Neck Slightly arched, moderate length, very muscular and almost equal to the skull in circumference.

Forequarters Chest, wide and deep well set down between forelegs, with deep brisket; shoulders muscular, sloping and powerful, not overloaded; pasterns straight and strong.

Body Girth and ribs, the girth may be up to one third more than the height of the dog. Ribs well sprung, deep and well set back to the hips, giving a rounded compact appearance.

Hindquarters Loins wide and muscular, with a fair depth of flank. Hind legs strong and muscular, with well-developed second thighs, denoting power and activity but not cumbersome. Hocks moderately bent. Cow hocks a definite fault.

Feet Not large, with rounded toes, well arched, cat feet, pads hard. Splay feet a decided fault.

Tail Set high, strong at root and tapering, reaching to the hocks, carried curved or straight, but not hound fashion. A visible crank undesirable, and a screw tail a fault.

Coat Short and dense, giving weather protection, lying flat to the body. A tendency to long, silken or woollen coat to be penalised.

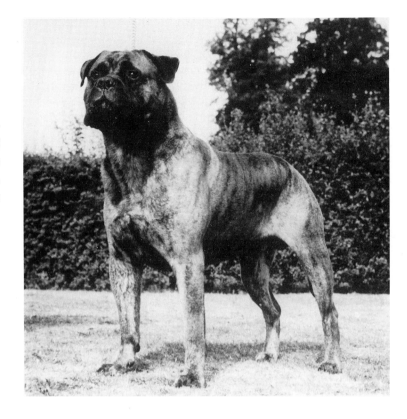

Ch. Clyde of Kelwall, bred by Lyn and Walter Pratt, owned by Mr and Mrs R.G. Snell: Widely recognised as a top-class specimen of the breed.

Colour Any shade of brindle, fawn or red, but the colour to be pure and clear. A white marking on chest permissible. Other white markings a definite fault. A black muzzle is preferable, toning off towards the eyes with dark markings round the eyes, giving expression.

Weight and Size Dogs should be 25 to 27 ins. at the shoulder and a 100 to 130 lbs in weight. Bitches should be 24 to 26 ins. at the shoulder, and 90 to 110 lbs in weight. It must be borne in mind that size must be proportionate with weight, and soundness and activity is most essential.

From 1956 onwards, there were quite a number of minor changes to the British Breed Standard. The fourth edition, as issued by the Kennel Club in March 1994, follows.

BRITISH BREED STANDARD

GENERAL APPEARANCE Powerful build, symmetrical, showing great strength, but not cumbersome; sound and active.

CHARACTERISTICS Powerful, enduring, active and reliable.

TEMPERAMENT High-spirited, alert and faithful.

HEAD AND SKULL Skull large and square, viewed from every angle, fair wrinkle when

interested, but not when in repose. Circumference of skull may equal height of dog when measured at top of shoulder; broad and deep with well filled cheeks. Pronounced stop. Muzzle short; distance from tip of nose to stop, approximately one third of length from tip of nose to centre of occiput, broad under eyes and sustaining nearly same width to end of nose; blunt and cut off square, forming right angle with upper line of face, and at same time proportionate with skull. Under jaw broad to end. Nose broad with widely spreading nostrils; flat, neither pointed nor turned up in profile. Flews not pendulous, never hanging below level of lower jaw.

EYES Dark or hazel, of medium size, set apart the width of the muzzle with furrow between. Light or yellow eyes highly undesirable.

EARS V shaped, folded back, set on wide and high, level of occiput giving square appearance to skull which is most important. Small and deeper in colour than body. Point of ear level with eye when alert. Rose ears are highly undesirable.

MOUTH Level desired but slightly undershot allowed but not preferred. Canine teeth large and set wide apart, other teeth strong, even and well placed.

NECK Well arched, moderate length, very muscular and almost equal to skull in circumference.

FOREQUARTERS Chest, wide and deep, well let down between forelegs, with deep brisket. Shoulders muscular, sloping and powerful, not overloaded. Forelegs powerful and straight, well-boned, set wide apart, presenting a straight front. Pasterns straight and strong.

BODY Back short and straight, giving compact carriage, but not so short as to interfere with movement. Roach and sway backs highly undesirable.

HINDQUARTERS Loins wide and muscular with fair depth of flank. Hindlegs strong, and muscular, with well developed second thighs, denoting power and activity, not cumbersome. Hocks moderately bent. Cowhocks highly undesirable.

FEET Well arched, cat-like, with rounded toes, pads hard. Dark toenails desirable. Splay feet highly undesirable.

TAIL Set high, strong at root and tapering, reaching to hocks, carried straight or curved, but not hound fashion. Crank tails highly undesirable.

GAIT/MOVEMENT Movement indicates power and strength of purpose. When moving straight, neither front nor hindlegs should cross or plait, right front and left rear legs rising and falling at the same time. A firm backline unimpaired by powerful thrust from hindlegs denoting a balanced and harmonious movement.

COAT Short and hard, weather resistant, lying flat to body. Long, silky or woolly coats highly undesirable.

COLOUR Any shade of brindle, fawn or red, colour to be pure and clear. A slight white marking on chest permissible. Other white markings undesirable. Black muzzle essential, toning off towards eyes, with dark markings around eyes contributing towards expression.

SIZE Height at shoulder: dogs 63.5-68.5 cms. (25-27 ins.); bitches 61-66 cms. (24-26 ins.). Weight: dogs 50-90 kgs. (110-130 lbs.); bitches 41-50 kgs. (90-110 lbs.).

FAULTS Any departure from the foregoing points should be considered a fault and the seriousness with which the fault should be regarded should be in exact proportion to its degree.

NOTE Male animals should have two apparently normal testicles fully descended into the scrotum.
Reproduced by kind permission of the Kennel Club.

The American Kennel Club approved the most recent Breed Standard for the Bullmastiff in February 1992. It is as follows:

AMERICAN BREED STANDARD

GENERAL APPEARANCE That of a symmetrical animal, showing great strength, endurance and alertness, powerfully built but active. The foundation breeding was 60% Mastiff and 40% Bulldog. The breed was developed in England by gamekeepers for protection against poachers.

SIZE, PROPORTION, SUBSTANCE Size. Dogs 25 to 27 ins. at the withers, and 110 to 130 lbs. weight. Bitches 24 to 26 ins. at the withers, and 100 to 120 lbs. weight. Other things being equal, the more substantial dog within these limits is favoured. Proportion. The length from tip of breastbone to rear of thigh exceeds the height from withers to ground only slightly, resulting in a nearly square appearance.

HEAD Expression. Keen, alert and intelligent. Eyes. Dark and of medium size. Ears. V shaped and carried close to the cheeks, set on wide and high, level with occiput and cheeks, giving a square appearance to the skull, darker in colour than the body and medium in size. Skull. Large, with a fair amount of wrinkle when alert; broad, with cheeks well developed. Forehead. Flat. Stop. Moderate. Muzzle. Broad and deep, its length, in comparison with that of the entire head, approximately as 1 is to 3. Lack of foreface with nostrils set on top of muzzle is a reversion to the Bulldog and is very undesirable. A dark muzzle is preferable. Nose. Black, with nostrils large and broad. Flews. Not too pendulous. Bite. Preferably level or slightly undershot. Canine teeth large and set wide apart.

NECK, TOPLINE, BODY Neck. Slightly arched of moderate length, very muscular, and almost equal in circumference to the skull. Topline. Straight and level between withers and loin. Body. Compact. Chest wide and deep, with ribs well sprung and well set down between the forelegs. Back. Short, giving the impression of a well balanced dog. Loin. Wide, muscular and slightly arched, with fair depth of flank. Tail. Set on high, strong at the root, and tapering to the hocks. It may be straight or curved, but never carried hound fashion.

Am. Can. Ch. Shady Oak Dox Fetching Freida, owned by Dr and Mrs John Crawford: A multi all-breed Best in Show winner, nationally ranked in the US from 1993 to 1995.

FOREQUARTERS Shoulders muscular but not loaded, and slightly sloping. Forelegs straight, well-boned and set well apart, elbows turned neither in nor out. Pasterns straight, feet of medium size, with round toes well arched. Pads thick and tough, nails black.

HINDQUARTERS Broad and muscular, with well-developed second thigh denoting power, but not cumbersome. Moderate angulation at hocks. Cowhocks and splay feet are serious faults.

COAT Short and dense, giving good weather protection.

COLOR Red, fawn or brindle. Except for a very small white spot on the chest, white marking is considered a fault.

GAIT Free, smooth and powerful. When viewed from the side, reach and drive indicate maximum use of the dog's moderate angulation. Back remains level and firm. Coming and going, the dog moves in a straight line. Feet tend to converge under the body, without crossing over, as speed increases. There is no twisting in or out at the joints.

TEMPERAMENT Fearless and confident yet docile. The dog combines the reliability, intelligence, and willingness to please required in a dependable family companion and protector.
Reproduced by kind permission of the American Kennel Club.

At the present time the FCI accepts the UK Standard. Australia and New Zealand have the same Standard, but moves are afoot to include disqualifying faults into the New Zealand Breed Standard.

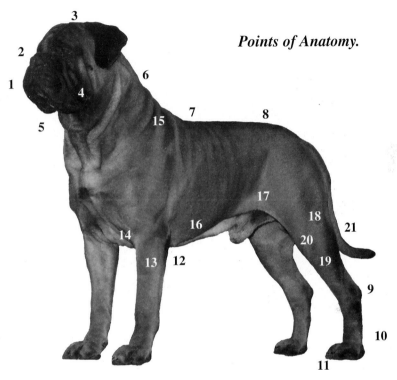

Points of Anatomy.

KEY

1. Muzzle	*8. Loin*	*15. Shoulder*
2. Stop	*9. Hock*	*16. Ribs*
3. Occiput	*10. Pasterns*	*17. Flank*
4. Cheek	*11. Toes*	*18. First thigh*
5. Dewlap	*12. Point of Elbow*	*19. Second thigh*
6. Arch of Neck	*13. Forearm*	*20. Stifle*
7. Withers	*14. Brisket*	*21. Tail*

INTERPRETATION OF THE BREED STANDARDS

The UK Standard has taken almost seventy years to reach its present state. To follow its development, I have given you the UK Standards as put forward in 1926, 1943, 1956 and 1994. I do not know when the Breed Standard was first drawn up in America.

GENERAL APPEARANCE, CHARACTERISTICS AND TEMPERAMENT

These points are glossed over in the UK Standard but the US Standard stresses the Bullmastiff's origin, its original usage and its value today as a companion and family protector.

Correct head and skull, with typical expression.

Gordon vom Antoniushof: The black mask is regarded as an important feature of the breed.

HEAD AND SKULL

If you talk to the average exhibitor, the head is the only part of the Bullmastiff which is of any importance. The UK Standard says the skull must be large and square, suggesting that its circumference may equal the height of the dog at the shoulder i.e. 25 to 27 ins. All that is asked for in the US Standard is that it be large. Both are agreed that there should be some wrinkle when the dog is alert or interested *but not when it is in repose.* There is almost complete agreement on the length of muzzle: approximately one third of the length from the tip of the nose to the occiput. In the UK Standard it must be broad and deep and cut off to form a right angle with the upper line of the face. Against this there is agreement about breadth and width, with the proviso that the nostrils must not be set on top, giving the resemblance to a Bulldog. There is a difference of opinion on the 'Stop', which is 'pronounced' in the UK Standard and 'moderate' in the other. In both cases it states that the flews must not be pendulous.

THE MUZZLE

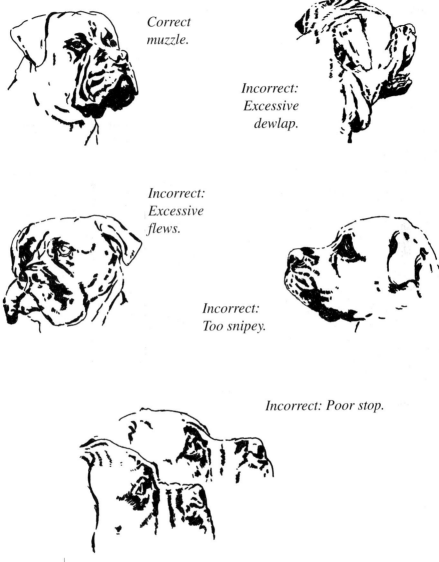

Correct muzzle.

Incorrect: Excessive dewlap.

Incorrect: Excessive flews.

Incorrect: Too snipey.

Incorrect: Poor stop.

Correct: Good stop.

EYES

Both Standards agree that they must be medium in size and the US Standard states that they should be dark. The UK Standard will also accept hazel and desires them to be set apart the width of the muzzle, with a furrow between. Perhaps this is the reason for the pronounced stop, which is a continuation of the furrow. The UK Standard also dislikes light or yellow eyes.

EARS

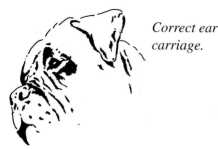

Correct ear carriage.

Incorrect ear carriage.

EARS

With so much emphasis laid on the head, I am appalled to see that neither Standard clarifies the setting of the ears. Over the years I have tried to persuade the UK Breed Council to do something, but the latest Standard is the worst yet -- "V shaped, folded back". I have yet to find a judge who does not penalise a dog whose ears are not folded forward. The usual critique is "fails in ear carriage". While the UK accepts "set on wide and high, level of occiput giving square appearance to the skull", the US Standard states: "V shaped and carried close to the cheeks, set on wide and high, level with occiput and cheeks, giving a square appearance to the skull". To me, the latter gives way to the Mastiff Standard where the ears lie close to the cheeks when the animal is in repose. There is a difference in size also, as the UK asks for "small ears", against "medium ears" in the US Standard. The Standards agree on colour "deeper or darker in colour than the rest of the body". When a Bullmastiff is interested, there is a visible reaction – the ears will be tightened and the point of the ear will be level with point of the eye. Some judges will click their fingers or shake a bunch of keys to obtain this effect. Sad to say, some judges, when assessing a dog's head, will pull the ears forward towards the point of the eyes. When questioned, they usually say, "I am measuring the length of the ears". This is odd, because there is no mention of length in the Standard.

MOUTH

In the UK Standard "Level desired but slightly undershot allowed. Canine teeth large and set wide apart, other teeth strong, even and well placed", while in the US Standard it is referred to as "bite" but there is no mention of "other teeth". Here again, I feel that the breed everywhere would benefit if more attention was given to "mouth" or "bite". Many breeders and exhibitors stress the fact that the Bullmastiff is said to be a 'head' breed and yet so little thought is given to the mouth. Breeding for a level mouth often sacrifices width of muzzle. Of the twenty-seven breeds in the latest list of the KC's Working Group, twenty-three desire or prefer a level mouth; one does not mention dentition and the three remaining are the Boxer, the Bullmastiff and the Mastiff. The Boxer requires an undershot jaw; the Bullmastiff says "level desired but slightly undershot allowed". The Mastiff, to my mind, gives a much clearer picture and I feel it would be good for the Bullmastiff to adopt the same Standard – "Canine teeth healthy, powerful and wide apart; incisors level or lower projecting beyond upper but never so much as to become visible when the mouth is closed".

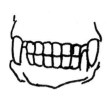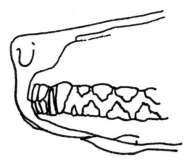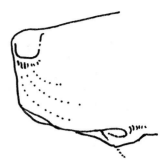

THE MOUTH

TOP: Correct level bite viewed from the front and side.

RIGHT: Level bite

FAR RIGHT: Scissor bite

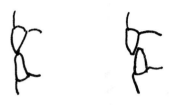

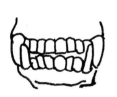

Incorrect: Undershot mouth viewed from the front and side.

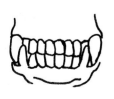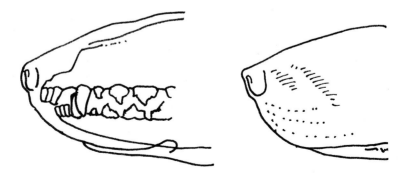

Incorrect: Overshot mouth viewed from the front and side.

NECK
The only difference in this section is on the "well arched" of the UK Standard and the "slightly arched" of the US Standard.

FOREQUARTERS
The emphasis is mainly on the chest being wide and deep, and well let down between the forelegs. From the side, the base line of the chest should be around the point of the elbow. The UK Standard refers to deep brisket, while the US Standard states that the ribs are well sprung. Shoulders could present a problem because the UK Standard states that they must be muscular, sloping and powerful and not overloaded; while the US version states that they should be muscular but not loaded, and slightly sloping. It's the difference between sloping and slightly sloping which is of importance. There is nothing worse than a Bullmastiff which is too straight in shoulder. Overloaded shoulders are ugly and cumbersome. Although both Standards agree on straight forelegs, the US Standard stresses that the elbows should turn neither in nor out. Quite often the elbows turn out when the shoulders are overloaded. There is complete agreement on good, straight pasterns.

Bunsoro Buckley (Kingsreach the Navigator of Murbisa – Sorrel Bachanalia of Bunsoro), owned by Susan Bennett. This powerfully-built dog shows well-constructed forequarters.

Photo: John Jackson.

FOREQUARTERS

LEFT: Incorrect: shallow brisket.
RIGHT: Correct: Good depth of brisket.

LEFT: Incorrect: Too straight in shoulders.
RIGHT: Correct: Shoulders well laid back.

BODY

The UK concern is mainly with the back, while the Americans include the chest, which has been covered in the section on forequarters. The back should be short, but not too short. Roach and sway backs are to be avoided. If the back is too short, movement is impeded. The hind legs are forced to move outside the front legs to avoid contact. Either that, or the dog will "crab"; that is to say, the hind legs will move to the side of the forelegs. If the back is too long, there is a tendency for it to dip or sag in the middle.

THE BODY

LEFT: Incorrect: Saddle back.
RIGHT: Incorrect: Roach back.

HINDQUARTERS

*Correct
hindquarters.*

HINDQUARTERS

Here there is complete agreement – strength and power with well-developed second thigh. I confess that I am concerned that neither Standard includes the avoidance of straight stifles, which are fast becoming a common feature, in the UK at any rate. This is the main reason why today's exhibitors in the UK tend to show their dogs 'head on' instead of sideways. Some exhibitors are resentful when asked to present their dog sideways.

*Incorrect:
Sickle-
legged.*

*Incorrect:
Cow hocks.*

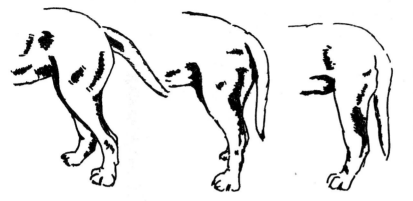

LEFT: Correct stifles and hocks.
CENTRE: Incorrect: straight hock.
RIGHT: Incorrect: straight stifle.

FEET AND TAIL

I have put these together because both Standards are easy to understand. The US Standard almost gives the impression that the fore-feet are different from the hind-feet. The UK scores here because it does not differentiate. The tail often causes concern for some judges if it is raised above the level of the back when the dog is on the move. The Standard requires a high set tail which means that the tail is lifted when the dog begins to move out. When the dog is stationary, the tail returns to its normal position. Looking back at the section in Chapter One dealing with Canis Urcani – the Mastiffs, it states that the tails were carried erect. As this section includes the English Mastiff and the Bull-dog I would be interested to know whether it was man or nature who decided how the tail should be carried.

TAIL CARRIAGE

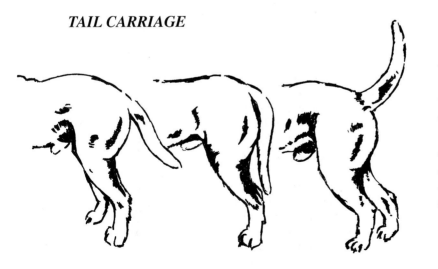

LEFT AND CENTRE: Correct tail carriage.

RIGHT: Incorrect: Gay tail (when moving).

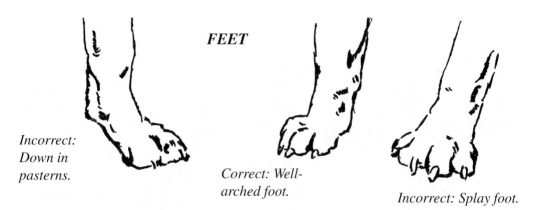

FEET

Incorrect: Down in pasterns.

Correct: Well-arched foot.

Incorrect: Splay foot.

GAIT/MOVEMENT

It is very important to look at the elbows and hocks when the dog is on the move. The former often turn out and the later turn in, giving anything but smooth, strong, movement. The dog should move straight and, if built correctly, the legs should not cross or plait. It is essential that the left hind leg follows the right front leg and vice versa, thus maintaining balance. A clever handler will find the right pace for the dog so as to maintain smooth, harmonious movement. If the dog is moved too slowly, both right front and right rear leg will move in unison, giving an awkward, ungainly movement. A dog who is moved too quickly will break into a gallop. The front legs will move out together. Again, the movement is ungainly, as the back arches and stretches. It is unfortunate that the UK Standard states "right front and left rear leg rising and falling at the same time'. It would have been better to say "moving forward", as "rising and falling" gives the impression of hackney movement.

COAT AND COLOUR

The UK Standard is the one to aim for as it is far more explicit than the US Standard. Strange as it may seem, the colouring of the muzzle is dismissed so lightly in the US Standard that it comes with the section on head – *a dark muzzle is preferable.* Over the years, as the UK Standard has been revised, it has changed "dark mask/muzzle desirable" to "dark mask/muzzle essential" and, finally, to "*black mask/muzzle essential,* toning off towards the eyes, with dark markings around the eyes contributing to expression". This is the icing on the cake and I feel so sad if it is being ignored or treated casually.

SIZE

Here again there are differences. A casual glance gives height and weight as being the same, but the American height is taken at the withers, which are slightly higher than the shoulders. This should mean that the American Bullmastiff may be a little leaner than the UK counterpart. I am not happy with the proviso from America – "Other things being equal, the more substantial dog within those limits favoured". Does this mean that a good big dog should be placed above an equally good, smaller dog, when both are within the Standard? This denotes a feeling for the Mastiff element and it does not tally with the Standard drawn up by the Southern Bullmastiff Society and Training Club in 1943 – "A refined type, not to be confused with either the Bulldog or the Mastiff".

Chapter Seven

THE SHOW RING

Your puppy is now six months old and is developing along the right lines, with a good, shiny coat, bright eyes and a friendly disposition. For the past six weeks you have both been along to ring training classes and people there have suggested that it might be a good idea to enter a show.

GETTING STARTED
Where do you begin? In the ring training classes your dog will have been mixing with all breeds and sizes of dogs. There may be a canine society in your vicinity which is running an open show. The number of choices of classes available will depend on the size of the society. A small society will have a class for Any Variety (AV) Minor Puppy. This caters for any puppy between six and

The road to success: Bunsoro Black Bessie, aged nine months, awarded Best Puppy in Show at the Joint Bullmastiff and Mastiff Show in Sweden, 1994.

nine months of age. If it is a big society, there may be a class for AV Working (Wkg) MP. This caters for any puppy in the Working Group between six and nine months of age. It may be that there are no classes for MP, in which case there may be a Puppy Class, catering for puppies between six and twelve months of age. Showing can be a very expensive business. Apart from entry fees, you may be asked to join the society and you will then be asked to buy raffle tickets etc., which will help to boost the society's funds. If it is a local show, transport will be comparatively cheap. And there you have it – before you "dive in at the deep end, dip your toes in the water nearer home". On the credit side, you will meet people from different walks of life. You may build up friendships which will be invaluable in the years ahead. Your puppy may prove to be a natural showman with great potential, in which case, you go ahead. If your little cygnet proves in reality to be a bit of an ugly duckling, stay with your local society where you and your dog can still have lots of fun, without paying out a lot of money. Dog showing should be fun for you and your dog. When it is no longer fun, it is time to stay at home. Your feelings are transferred along the lead to the dog. If you are in a bad mood, do not blame the dog if you do not win a place. Remember, if you really love your dog, you always take the best dog home.

TYPES OF SHOWS IN THE UK

If you have decided that dog showing is for you, your next step is to join the Breed Club nearest to you. There are six clubs serving England, Scotland and Wales. Each club usually sends out show schedules and newsletters. A good newsletter will also carry details of the major championship shows – the date, the venue and the name of the judge. All recognised shows are run subject to the rules and regulations of the Kennel Club. Until recently there were Championship, Open, Limited and Sanction Shows, but now we have Primary Shows as well. A Primary Show may be the one for you, if you are an absolute beginner. No dog which has won a First Prize at any Show (Puppy, Special Puppy, Minor Puppy and Special Minor Puppy classes excepted), CC or Reserve CC may compete at a Primary Show. Entries may be taken on the day of the Show, but the dog must be eligible for the Show at the time of entry.

   Sanction Shows scheduling one breed may provide up to ten classes, which must include a Postgraduate Class; and a show scheduling more than one breed may provide up to twenty-five classes, which must include a Postgraduate Class for each breed. Limited Shows are limited to members of the club or society running the show and dogs which have won a CC, or its equivalent, are not eligible for entry. There must be a minimum of twelve classes, which must include an Open Class. Open Shows are, as the name implies, open to any dog, while Championship Shows are open to any dog with the proviso that the ultimate winner may progress to becoming a breed champion.

   Just to help you in your choice of classes, I have included the following definitions: * applies to Championship and Open Shows only; ** applies to Limited, Sanction and Primary Shows only. Where there is no qualification, the Definition applies to all types of Shows. In estimating the number of awards won, all wins up to and including the seventh day before the date of closing of entries shall be counted when entering for any class. Wins in Variety Classes do not count for entry in Breed Classes, but when entering for Variety Classes, wins in both Breed and Variety Classes must be counted. A First Prize does not include a Special Prize of whatever value.

Minor puppy For dogs of six and not exceeding nine calendar months of age on the first day of the Show.
Puppy For dogs of six and not exceeding twelve calendar months of age on the first day of the Show.

Junior For dogs of six and not exceeding eighteen calendar months of age on the first day of the Show.

Beginners *For owner, handler or exhibit not having won a first prize at a Championship or Open Show.

**For owner, handler or exhibit not having won a first prize at any Show.

Maiden *For dogs which have not won a Challenge Certificate or a First Prize at an Open or Championship Show (Minor Puppy, Special Minor Puppy, Puppy and Special Puppy classes excepted, whether restricted or not).

**For dogs which have not won a First Prize at any Show (Minor Puppy, Special Minor Puppy, Puppy and Special Puppy classes excepted, whether restricted or not).

Novice *For dogs which have not won a Challenge Certificate or three or more First Prizes at Open and Championship Shows (Minor Puppy, Special Minor Puppy, Puppy and Special Puppy classes excepted, whether restricted or not).

**For dogs which have not won three or more First Prizes at any Show (Minor Puppy, Special Minor Puppy, Puppy and Special Puppy classes excepted, whether restricted or not).

Tyro *For dogs which have not won a Challenge Certificate or five or more First Prizes at Open and Championship Shows (Minor Puppy, Special Minor Puppy, Puppy and Special Puppy classes excepted, whether restricted or not).

**For dogs which have not won five or more First Prizes at any Show (Minor Puppy, Special Minor Puppy, Puppy and Special Puppy classes excepted, whether restricted or not).

Débutant *For dogs which have not won a Challenge Certificate or a First Prize at a Championship Show (Minor Puppy, Special Minor Puppy, Puppy and Special Puppy classes excepted, whether restricted or not).

**For dogs which have not won a First Prize at an Open or Championship Show (Minor Puppy, Special Minor Puppy, Puppy and Special Puppy classes excepted, whether restricted or not).

Undergraduate *For dogs which have not won a Challenge Certificate or three or more First Prizes at Championship Shows (Minor Puppy, Special Minor Puppy, Puppy and Special Puppy classes excepted, whether restricted or not).

**For dogs which have not won three or more First Prizes at Open or Championship Shows (Minor Puppy, Special Minor Puppy, Puppy and Special Puppy classes excepted, whether restricted or not).

Graduate *For dogs which have not won a Challenge Certificate or four or more First Prizes at Championship Shows in Graduate, Postgraduate, Minor Limit, Mid Limit, Limit and Open classes, whether restricted or not.

**For dogs which have not won four or more First Prizes at Open or Championship Shows in Graduate, Postgraduate, Minor Limit, Mid Limit, Limit and Open classes, whether restricted or not.

Postgraduate *For dogs which have not won a Challenge Certificate or five or more First Prizes at Championship Shows in Postgraduate, Minor Limit, Mid Limit, Limit and Open classes, whether restricted or not.

**For dogs which have not won five or more First Prizes at Championship and Open Shows in Postgraduate, Minor Limit, Mid Limit, Limit and Open classes, whether restricted or not.

Minor limit *For dogs which have not won two Challenge Certificate or three or more First prizes in all at Championship Shows in Minor Limit, Mid Limit, Limit and Open classes, confined to the breed, whether restricted or not, at Shows where Challenge Certificates were offered for the breed.

**For dogs which have not won three or more First Prizes in all at Open and Championship Shows in Minor Limit, Mid Limit, Limit and Open classes, confined to the breed, whether restricted or not.

Mid limit *For dogs which have not won three Challenge Certificates or five or more First Prizes in all at Championship Shows in Mid Limit, Limit and Open classes, confined to the breed, whether restricted or not, at Shows where Challenge Certificates were offered for the breed.
**For dogs which have not won five or more First Prizes in all at Open and Championship Shows in Mid Limit, Limit and Open classes, confined to the breed, whether restricted or not.
Limit *For dogs which have not won three Challenge Certificates under three different judges or seven or more First Prizes in all, at Championship Shows in Limit and Open classes, confined to the breed, whether restricted or not, at Shows where Challenge Certificates were offered for the breed.
**For dogs which have not won seven or more First Prizes in all at Open and Championship Shows in Limit and Open classes, confined to the breed, whether restricted or not.
Open For all dogs of the breeds for which the class is provided and eligible for entry at the Show.

Wins at Championship shows in breed classes where Challenge Certificates are not on offer shall be counted as wins at Open shows.

There you have it – a very brief outline of the show scene in the UK. If your puppy is successful in the early shows, then you may decide to take up showing in a serious way. Unless you have unlimited financial resources, you would be well advised to work your way through each class, passing on when you have made the necessary wins. When each class of dogs has been judged, all the unbeaten dogs are called into the ring. From these the judge will select the best dog, or in the case of a Championship Show, the DCC. Before judging the bitches, the reserve dog or the Reserve DCC must be selected. This may be one of the remaining unbeaten dogs, or it may be the dog which has only been beaten by the best dog or the DCC. Thus it can be seen that the Best of Sex need not be the Winner of the Open Class. The same procedure is carried out for the bitches. The judge, having selected best bitch or BCC, must also select a reserve. From the best of each sex, the best of breed is selected. Here again, the judge must also select a reserve. It may be the Best Opposite Sex or the Reserve Dog or Bitch beaten by the BoB. We have not finished yet – the judge must select the Best Puppy. This is the puppy which has not been beaten by any other puppy. This sometimes causes problems when a puppy comes forward which has not been entered in a Puppy Class. However, it is still unbeaten by another puppy. From the BPD and BPB the judge selects the BP. In the event of a puppy winning Best of Sex and the CC or the Reserve BoS and the Reserve CC, there will be no further judging for BP. The first CC sets you off on the path for further success. For your dog to become a champion, it must be awarded three CCs under three different judges. There is an unwritten rule, or a gentleman's agreement, that a dog is not shown under its breeder. The KC rulings are that a dog must not have been registered or owned by the judge within twelve months prior to the show (this does not apply if the judge is appointed in an emergency). Neither must it have been boarded or prepared for exhibition within the previous twelve months by the judge (this again does not apply if the judge is appointed in an emergency).

TYPES OF SHOWS IN THE USA
There are two major types of dog shows, Specialty and All-breed Shows. There are also Match Shows, which are usually judged by those who are aspiring to become Championship Show judges. Classes usually range from Puppy through Novice and Post-graduate to Open. Champions are not eligible for Matches. The Specialty Shows are limited to dogs of a specific breed or grouping of breeds. All-breeds Shows are open to over one hundred and thirty breeds recognised by the AKC. The actual system of showing is far different from the system in the UK, although the final aim is the same – to make your dog into a Champion, carry on to go Best of Breed, and then Best in Show. Most of the dogs in shows are seeking to win points towards their title of Champion.

Showing American style: Am. Ch. Tundra's Pinewood Baron ROM, OFA: Best of Breed at the 1990 ABA National from the Veteran class.

This means that the dog must win fifteen points including two 'majors'. A 'major' is a win of three, four or five points. These points must be won under at least three different judges. A dog can win from one to five points, according to the number of dogs competing in each breed. There are six regular classes in which a dog can be entered: Puppy, Twelve to Eighteen Months, Novice, Bred by Exhibitor, American-Bred, and Open.

After these six classes are judged, the class winners compete for best of the first place dogs. This is done for each sex. Only the Winners Dog and the Winners Bitch receive Championship points. (A Reserve Winner award is given in each sex to the runner up.) At this point, the Winners Dog and the Winners Bitch compete with the champions for Best of Breed.

At the end of the BoB judging, three awards are usually given:

Best of Breed – the dog judged as the best in its breed category

Best of Winners – the dog judged as best between Winners Dog and Winners Bitch.

Best of Opposite Sex – the dog that is the opposite sex of the BoB winner.

Each BoB winner goes forward to compete in one of the seven Groups. There are four placings in every Group but only the first in each Group goes forward to compete for the Best in Show.

There are two very interesting points here. An up-and-coming dog can become a Champion without having to compete against other Champions. The necessary points are won before they come up against the Champions, although additional points may be earned if the class dog defeats a Champion. Championship points are awarded according to the number of dogs which are present at the show. The more dogs present and beaten, the higher the number of points awarded – five being the top number. In conclusion, once the status of Champion has been achieved, the dog can compete for BoB without having to win in the other classes.

PREPARING YOUR BULLMASTIFF FOR THE SHOW RING

It cannot be stressed too highly that the dog must be clean and free of any cosmetic preparations. The coat must be groomed so that there are no loose hairs. Check that the ears and the teeth are clean. As a judge, I hate to see a dog whose coat is really out of condition or a bitch who is in full season. A dog who develops a high temperature or a cough *must not be taken to the show.* Missing a show will not ruin your dog's career, but showing a dog with a high temperature or a cough, may injure other dogs and could prove fatal.

WHAT TO WEAR

Remember that you are there to show off the qualities of the dog. If your dog is a red or brindle, wear a light suit or dress, if fawn, wear a dark suit or dress. This gives the judge a chance to see the outline of the dog clearly. Make sure that whatever you wear is clean, and tidy, and does not draw the judge's attention away from the dog. Wear sensible shoes so that you can move the dog freely.

Ch. Dajean's Gold Dust The Poacher's Foe: Top bitch CC winner, owned by Ged and Jacqui Ling.
It is important to build up a good relationship with a show dog.

Photo: Carol Ann Johnson.

SHOW RING ETIQUETTE

Wherever in the world you are showing, there are basic manners to observe, whatever the details of the procedure, which can differ from country to country. Try to be at the ring side when your class number is called by the steward. Enter the ring quietly and collect your ring number from the steward. Fasten the ring number on your sleeve, where it can be clearly seen. If it is a big class, do not try to make your dog stand out of line in the hope that the judge will take special notice. Do not allow your dog to stand too close to the dog in front. If the judge asks for all dogs to be moved in a circle, do not try to overtake the dog in front. When the judge calls your dog forward, try to obey the judge's instructions. If the judge asks you to move in a triangle, remember that a triangle consists of three straight sides and three corners. If you cannot or will not move your dog in a straight line, a good judge may penalise your dog. The object of the exercise is to assess movement. When the judge has examined your dog etc., go to your place at the end of the line, unless directed otherwise. Unless you are the last to be seen, try to allow your dog to relax while the other dogs are being judged.

When all the dogs in the class have been judged, prepare your dog for the final assessment. Do not try to move your dog forward; be fair to the other exhibitors. Try to leave a space between you and the dogs on either side of you. Over the past few years some exhibitors have begun to stretch out the dog's hind legs. This is not for the Bullmastiff. The dog who is built correctly, with a level back, will stand square. It is permissible to move the forelegs so that they are not too close together. Try not to string the head too high. Move into line, or out of the ring, when you are told to do so by the judge or steward. Winning or losing, remember that as far as you are concerned, you have the best dog there. Wherever you are placed, give your dog lots of praise. A good dog can be spoiled by over-handling. If your dog is beaten, do not forget to congratulate the winner. The situations may be reversed at the next show!

Lyn Pratt judging Bullmastiffs: Honesty is the key word when you are invited to judge the breed. Photo: J.K. & E.A. McFarlane.

THE JUDGE'S ROLE

How better to begin this section than with a few words of advice from Shakespeare's *Hamlet*? They were given to Laertes by his father, Polonius. "This above all – to thine own self be true; and it must follow, as the night the day, thou canst not then be false to any man." When you enter the show ring, all eyes are upon you. It is in your power to make some people happy and some people angry. If it is a Championship show you may be responsible for awarding a dog its first CC, the first step towards making the dog into a Champion. If you honestly feel that an unknown dog is the best dog there, be brave, award that dog the CC. It is so easy to follow in another judge's footsteps and think, "That one must be good because So-and-so awarded that dog the CC last month." If the current favourite does not, in your eyes, fit the breed standard, do not be afraid to mark that dog down. Judge the dogs and not the exhibitors. The same applies to Open and Limited Shows.

THE JUDGE'S RESPONSIBILITIES

The judge must try to be in the judging ring at least ten minutes before judging is due to commence, thus providing the time to meet the stewards. Together, they can discuss where the seen and unseen dogs are to be placed and also where the winning dogs can be placed. The final decision is made by the judge who, if there is any 'comeback' after the show, must shoulder the responsibility. Nowadays all absentees must be noted and entered in the judge's book. Check the judge's table to see that the judge's book and the principal award cards or ribbons are there. Each page must be signed by the judge. This means that there must be a good working relationship between the stewards and the judge, if mistakes are to be avoided. Once you are satisfied that everything is in order, you can ask your stewards to call the first class into the ring. I say 'ask', because politeness must be the order of the day. If you are polite to your stewards, they will be polite to the exhibitors.

SUITABLE CLOTHING

As a judge your attire must be as neat and tidy as possible. If you are a man, try to wear a suit with a collar and tie. Jeans are fine for casual wear, but you are the judge and you must look the part. Try to avoid heavy after-shave. If you are a woman remember that you have to bend down to get a closer look at the puppies. Avoid short skirts, tight skirts and low-necked dresses or blouses. A well-cut trouser suit, or a well fitted pair of slacks with a blouse, is always acceptable. Avoid hats, if at all possible. As a breed, the average Bullmastiff hates hats and will back away from the judge who is wearing one. Try to avoid jangling jewellery or anything that will distract the dog's attention. Unless you always wear high heels, wear sensible shoes so that you can change your position quickly. Again, try to avoid the use of heavy perfume or hand cream. Dogs in general have a very keen sense of smell.

ORGANISING THE RING

On the day of the show a quick look at the judge's book will give you an idea of the number of dogs entered in each class. A club or Specialty show usually draws a good entry and it may be necessary to split a class in half, so that there is sufficient room to move each individual dog. Try to persuade spectators to keep their dogs well clear of the ring, if they are not in the current class. If at all possible, try to position yourself with your back to the sun so that you can see the movement of every dog. Do not allow one exhibitor to block out another exhibitor's dog. Try to get the exhibitors to use every inch of the ring so that you can see each dog clearly and the dogs are not too close for comfort and safety.

COMMON FAULTS TO LOOK FOR

The first part of a dog which you examine is the head. Look at the eyes: they should be dark brown, medium size, and clean. Sticky eyelids *may* denote entropion. Light eyes are not acceptable. The muzzle should be broad. A long narrow muzzle must be avoided. While checking the muzzle, look at the teeth. Teeth should be large and in line. Very tiny teeth or irregular teeth are not acceptable. The underjaw must be broad and deep. A slightly undershot mouth is acceptable, but if you can get your fingers between upper and lower teeth, the mouth is bad. Stand back and look at the pigmentation. The muzzle should be black, toning off before the eyes. There should be black pencilling around the eyes. Too much black is as bad as too little. Snap your fingers and an alert Bullmastiff will show interest; the brow will wrinkle, causing the ears to fall forward. There should be very little wrinkle on the forehead of a Bullmastiff. Look at the dog's forelegs. They should be straight and the feet should be rounded, like a cat's. The toe nails should preferably be black. The bone must not be too fine or too coarse. The neck must not be too short, nor too long. It must not be too thin and it must be gently arched. A narrow, shallow chest is easy to see and must be avoided. The shoulders must not be too upright or overloaded. The back must be short and straight, leading into a high-set tail. A long back and a low set tail must be avoided. The tail should not be too thin or too cranked. Avoid, like the plague, straight stifles and weak undeveloped second thighs. Gentle pressure on the rear end should not upset the dog. If it is a male, you should be able to feel two testicles. Avoid long or woolly coats. The colour should be clear throughout. Excessive white is undesirable. Unfortunately this shows up more clearly on brindles and reds than it does on fawns, but it is still undesirable. Black should be confined to the head and toenails and perhaps the ears. Height and weight come in for much criticism. I maintain that a dog should be within the standard. Too tall or too heavy is just as bad as too small or too light.

Once you have made an individual examination of the dog indicate, as clearly as possible, the direction of movement. Some judges are content to see the dog move up and down the ring. This shows movement going away and returning. If the ring is big enough, the exhibitor must be asked to move the dog in a triangle. This shows movement going away, going across, and returning. With puppies, allowances must be made for erratic movement. It may be their first experience of the big ring and they are overwhelmed with all the noise. Sometimes it is very difficult to assess a puppy before asking the exhibitor to do the movement. In this case try again after the puppy has been moved. Whatever the age or size of the dogs, handle them gently. Rough handling may put a dog off showing for ever.

FINAL PLACINGS
Be decisive. Put up the dogs which you honestly believe are the best there. As a judge, you should have no friends and no enemies. The future of the breed owes a lot to the decisions of the judges. A true friend will accept an honest opinion. If you are thinking of becoming a judge, first become a steward. Try to steward for as many breed judges as possible. Look at the dogs they place and listen to what they say. If you show your own dogs, look at the judge's critiques. See why you think your own dog won or lost. It's not easy being a judge. When you are in the ring you can see things which the ringsider does not see – particularly the eyes and the mouths. Do not rush into it. Rome was not built in a day and a judge is not made in a couple of years.

Chapter Eight

BREEDING AND REARING

Why do you want to breed Bullmastiffs? You must consider the following questions very carefully before you proceed any further. Have you got a really good dog or bitch whose bloodlines you would like to continue? Would you be able to find good homes for the puppies which you did not wish to keep? Could you keep all the puppies which you could not sell? Could you afford to feed the stud dog, the brood bitch and the puppies with the balanced diet which is essential? If you can honestly answer 'yes' to all these questions you should be able to proceed, but there are other points to consider. Are you expecting to sell your puppies for six hundred to one thousand pounds, or equivalent currency? Perhaps you have heard that this is the going rate. If your kennel name is good enough, or you have the right contacts, you can do this. If not, you may have to sell your puppies for a much lower price and this often attracts buyers who can ill afford to keep a Bullmastiff. You can give away a puppy from a small breed quite easily to good owners, but you must find a suitable home for a Bullmastiff. Always remember, a Bullmastiff will grow into a big dog and in the growing stages will consume plenty of good food.

  The final points often cause more trouble and heart-break than anything else. Do you own the stud dog or the brood bitch? The dog is yours. Good! That is one hurdle cleared. If he is not your dog, you are therefore intending to pay a stud fee. On the surface, this is good idea, but beware. If the bitch does not have any puppies there is no onus on the owner of a stud dog to provide a second service, unless it is written into the original agreement. Draw up a contract to be signed by you and the owner of the stud dog and ask beforehand if there is a second service if the bitch fails to whelp. Some stud dog owner may ask for a smaller stud fee with the pick of litter thrown in. Think carefully! There may only be one puppy. Your agreement is in writing and the stud dog owner is entitled to the puppy. However, he or she may be a decent person and may allow you to keep the puppy.

  If you own the bitch you must consider the points raised above. However, your bitch may be 'out on breeding terms'. This means different things to different people. I have never entered into any such agreement. In some cases a bitch puppy may be transferred to a new owner without payment. The breeder of the puppy will lay down his or her own conditions and these must be given careful consideration. It may be that when the bitch is old enough to breed from, her breeder will nominate the stud dog. Her breeder may also ask for more than one puppy, including the pick of the litter. If the bitch is on 'breeding terms', correctly speaking she is on loan. When it comes to registering the litter, the breeder will be the owner of the bitch at the time of whelping. This could mean that someone else will be credited with breeding your first litter or puppies. If it is a good litter, you may live to regret your agreement. Before you make any decision, try to find out at first hand what is really involved. Seek advice from someone who has had a bitch on 'breeding terms'.

After careful consideration, if you still wish to, go ahead. Everything, of course, must be put in writing so that, should a dispute arise between the parties involved, the matter can go to some form of official arbitration. Personally speaking, I would never accept a bitch on 'breeding terms' unless the agreement was registered at the UK Kennel Club. Beware of the owner of a bitch who refuses to make the transaction official. Do not fall into the trap of aiding and abetting a 'puppy farmer'. A genuine breeder/owner will be only too glad to tie up any loose ends.

BREEDING PROGRAMMES

Long before you decide that you are going to breed from your bitch, you must decide what you are looking for in the stud dog. Do not fall into the trap of going for the current winning dog. He may look good in the show ring, he may be just the type of dog you would like to own *but* – and it is a very big but – does his pedigree link up with that of your bitch? If it doesn't, think again. To the average person, breeding is easy. You follow a certain bloodline on a pedigree and then you bring in an 'outcross' on the third or fourth generation. If only it were as easy and straightforward as that, there would not be so many poor specimens on show.

When you look at a pedigree, look at the bitches as well as the dogs. Have you heard of them before? Do they belong to the same bloodlines as the dog? On many of today's pedigrees, every generation is an outcross as far as the bitches are concerned. Quite often the dog has been used at stud and a bitch puppy is taken in lieu of stud. The male line may consist of Champions bearing the same affix, but the bitches are as varied as the proverbial licorice allsorts, which is not favourable. On the other hand, a pedigree may carry the same affix on dogs and bitches and may, to all intents and purposes, be perfect line breeding. There is no sign of an outcross, but the line

Am. Ch. Charley Hexam ROM, bred and owned by Marjorie Triggs. This dog was a Best of Breed winner and has proved influential at stud. His name is found in the pedigrees of Tauralan, Bandog, and Aamodt Bullmastiffs.

Am. Can. Int. Ch. Blackslate's Boston Blackie, owned by Virginia Rowland and Mary B. Walsh. 'Mister' is the all-time top producer in the breed with a total of 41 American offspring. He was the first Bullmastiff to win an all-breed Best in Show in Spain and Portugal.

Ch. Bonnie of Kelwall: The first brindle Champion bred in the UK for 25 years. Bred and owned by Lyn and Walter Pratt.

Photo: F.E. Garwood.

breeding has not produced anything of quality. Why? Except for an odd mutation, nothing will come out of a litter which is not already in the bloodline. If you have used mediocre dogs and bitches you cannot expect good puppies. There are few lines today which are as pure as they were fifteen or twenty years ago. This makes breeding a bit of a gamble. If you find a dog which you like, look at his brothers and sisters, look at his offspring. Ask questions and try to store the information given. If the dogs and bitches which you see have many good points and few faults, all the better. What about your bitch? Has she got the same faults as the dog, his offspring and his litter mates? If she has, there is every chance that your puppies will have the same faults. In short, try to find a dog who is carrying as few faults as possible and try to ensure that your bitch does not carry the same faults. Do not be swayed by the number of Champions in a dog's pedigree unless you have some knowledge of those Champions, and of their contribution, if any, to the well-being of the breed. Remember, a dog is only as good as the offspring he produces. A Champion will be used at stud on many bitches, so more of his offspring will be on view. To date, two Champions have sired ten Champions each. One was born in 1929 and the other in 1943. Three champions have sired nine champions. One was born in 1944, one in 1962 and the other in 1983. Another dog who sired nine champions was born in 1970 but he himself did not win a single CC, thus proving the theory that the bloodlines are more important to a serious breeder than a list of prizes won.

Scyldocga Bullmast Bronwyn ROM and her Champion sons, Ch. Battersea of Bullmast and Ch. Bradbury of Bullmast. Bred by Mary Prescott.

THE BROOD BITCH

Before you consider mating your bitch, take her along to your vet for a thorough check-up. You must accept the vet's advice. If he says that her eyelids are suspect do not breed from her. Make sure that she is moving well, and have her X-rayed for HD. You may even decide to have her blood tested. If you want to have healthy puppies you must try, to the best of your ability, to ensure that she is free of hereditary faults. There is an old wife's tale that if your bitch has any faults, find a dog which does not have those faults – this will cancel them out. Do not believe it. You must have a brood bitch who is as near perfection as you can afford. You cannot get good puppies from bad stock. Make sure her inoculation programme is up to date and she has been properly wormed. If she is carrying too much weight, try to slim her down a little. Unless you are desperate to win a third CC, keep her out of the show ring in order to avoid the risk of any infection. Ideally, she should be around two years of age.

THE STUD DOG

Ideally, he too should have a clean bill of health. *Do not accept a dog because he is the current show winner.* Look at the stock he has produced. Look at his siblings. In other words, the stud dog must carry as few faults as possible. He, too, must not carry excess weight. It is a good idea to let him rest for a few days between stud services. You can do this if it is your own dog, but if he belongs to someone else, you accept this on trust.

MATING

This is, or should be, a natural process. Usually the bitch is taken to the dog. The actual date arranged for the mating seems to cause more trouble nowadays than it used to do years ago. One thing is certain: nature has the final word and a successful mating can only take place when the bitch is 'ready'. This varies from bitch to bitch, and also in subsequent matings with the same bitch. Some bitches have a regular cycle and it can safely be said when they will come into season. A good owner will have a record of all dates – worming, boosters, onset and cessation of season, etc. The average length of time between seasons is usually around six months but this is not the rule. Some bitches have their first season as early as six months of age, while others do not have their first season until they are ten months of age or more. It is important to check that the seasons are regular. If there is a wide variation, inform your vet. Quite often a bitch's attitude will begin to change a few days before her season is due to commence. She will become fussy and very affectionate. This is usually followed by a discharge from the vulva. It may be dark and bloody in colour, or it may be almost colourless. This makes it very difficult for the owner to observe, but as the vulva is normally swollen when the bitch is in season, this may be a guide. If the bitch is a house dog, it is unfair to turn her out of doors when she comes into season. Many pet shops now stock garments which can be worn during the season, so that there are no stains on the floor. Avoid the use of anti-dog sprays. I think they encourage dogs. If you have dogs, keep them away from the bitch. When you take the bitch outdoors, clean the area immediately with strong disinfectant.

As the discharge gets fainter and less frequent the vulva may become very soft and floppy. From about the ninth to tenth days stroke the area between the top of the leg and the vulva very gently. We have always relied on this. The vulva seems to develop a powerful thrust and it moves upwards. At the same time, the tail lifts and moves swiftly to one side. When this happens a few times it is usually an indication that the bitch is ready to accept the dog. It may be as early as the ninth day or it may be much later. This is why you cannot arrange a mating for a fixed date during the bitch's season. You can, of course, take your bitch along to the vet who will take a swab which should tell you when the bitch is ready for mating. This is not fool-proof either. All I can say is that if you want to avoid any clash of temperaments and wasted time and money, the mating must not be attempted until the bitch is ready. A forced mating may have a lasting effect on a bitch, bringing about a change of temperament. It may even make her aggressive towards other dogs. In some cases the bitch will resist all attempts at a mating and may even attack the dog. Please bear in mind that all dogs are not meant to be stud dogs, just as all bitches are not meant to be brood bitches. Nature is not perfect.

If the bitch is a maiden bitch, it is wise to use a proven stud dog, preferably one who is not rough in his approach. If the dog has not been used at stud before, he should be tried out on a proven bitch. If her previous mating ran smoothly, she will help the young dog along, teasing and tempting him. She will turn her vulva so that it is under the dog's nose in her attempts to teach him. It goes without saying that the dog and the bitch must be clean and healthy. I would never allow a mating between a dog and a bitch if either of them had a bad skin condition or running eyes, whatever the owner said. The area in which the mating is to take place must be spotlessly clean and large enough to allow freedom of movement. It must be light and airy and away from any disturbing noise or distraction. As the time taken for a mating can vary from fifteen minutes to three quarters of an hour or more, it is advisable to have two strong chairs or stools close at hand.

When the dog and the bitch are first introduced to each other they must be wearing collars with leads attached. This enables full control of the preliminaries. If either of them shows aggression they must be pulled away. Once it is obvious that there is a keen interest between dog and bitch, the leads can be removed. There may be a period of courtship, or the dog may decide to start work at once. He will attempt to mount the bitch and will clasp her round the body with his forelegs. After a few powerful thrusts, his penis will extend and it will enter the vulva. At this stage, the experienced breeder will be aware that the next stage may either be a 'tie' where the penis is held securely in place, or the penis may slip out. If it is the former, the dog's thrusting movements will cease and he may seem quite happy to stay where he is, astride the bitch. Gently, but firmly, move his legs so that he has all four legs on the ground, taking great care not to cause any irregular, jerky movements which may cause injury. At this point, opinions vary. Some breeders prefer to turn the dog and the bitch end to end so that they cannot bite each other. We have always allowed them to stand quietly, side by side. If the bitch has a low-set tail, it may be necessary to move it gently, so that it does not cause friction between the dog and the bitch. If the 'tie' lasts for any length of time, the owners or handlers of the dog and the bitch may sit down, but they must not allow either of the two animals to wriggle out of position, so they must keep holding onto the collars firmly. The dog may lick the bitch's ears and face during this period and vice-versa. Do not attempt to speed the process; allow nature to take its course. Do not allow the dog or the bitch to sit down or lie down, however hard they may try. This can be a tiring period for handlers and animals – so be prepared. When the 'tie' is over, the dog moves quietly away from the bitch and he may begin to clean himself. Wipe him down with a mild antiseptic. Wipe the bitch down too, and lead her away where she can rest for an hour or so.

If the penis slipped out during the initial thrust, it may mean that there was a 'slip mating' which could result in conception, or that the dog was over-eager. If it was the latter, separate the two for half an hour or more and then try again. If this happens a second time you must use your discretion. You can give both animals a long rest, away from each other, or you can call it a day. The attempted mating may have been too early or too late. Who knows? You can try again the following day, or the next season. This is what makes dog breeding so interesting – you can never foretell the outcome. A few words of warning before we leave this section. If you own the bitch, *never* let her out of your sight. The owner of the stud dog may try to persuade you that it will be better for all concerned if you are not there when the mating takes place. But if you are there, you will know the identity of the dog used.

PREPARATIONS FOR THE WHELPING

At least four weeks before the bitch is due to whelp, provision must be made for a whelping box. You may be able to borrow one, in which case it must be scrubbed clean and disinfected. If you make one, it must be made of strong wood approximately one inch or two point five centimetres thick. It must be approximately four feet or one hundred and twenty-five centimetres square. The sides must be approximately one foot three inches or forty centimetres high, and one side must be in two halves across the width. The two halves can be hinged on the outside, enabling the top half to be dropped down so that the bitch can get in and out with ease. Provision must be made for a 'pig rail' inside the box. This can be made from wood approximately two inches or five centimetres square. It must be approximately three inches or eight centimetres from the sides and the base of the box, and can be supported-in position by blocks screwed into the sides of the box. The use of the 'pig rail' saves the lives of many small puppies, who are pushed underneath it, out of harm's way, when the bitch moves round. Otherwise they can be squashed. During the actual whelping the box can be lined with sheets of newspaper which can be destroyed after use. When the last of the puppies is born, the box can be lined with veterinary bedding which must be changed daily. This type of bedding can be washed in the washing machine.

Once the whelping box is ready you must decide where the whelping is to take place. If you have a spare boxroom or bedroom, all the better. This makes observation so much easier, without the need to dash outdoors. Some of us prefer to have a camp bed or comfy armchair alongside the box, in which we can sleep, so that we can hear any signs of distress. Small puppies are very vulnerable, especially if the litter is a large one. The bitch hears a squeal from a puppy which has strayed away and, in her haste and anxiety to reach the puppy, she may stand on one of the others. If you, or your 'stand in', hear the cry, you are close at hand to offer assistance. The box must be in a draught-free situation and it must be at least one inch or two point five centimetres away from the floor. The room must be warm, and if possible, an infra-red lamp or 'pig lamp' must be suspended over the box. It must be high enough to keep the air above the box warm, but not so low as to cause distress to the puppies. The bitch, being nearer to the lamp, will feel the heat more, but she can move out of the immediate range. It is also a good idea to have a supply of sterile gauze, or well-boiled white cloth at hand. You may need it to hold a puppy who is in difficulty. One or two hot-water bottles and cardboard boxes lined with clean pieces of blanket or veterinary bedding will also prove useful if it is a lengthy whelping or a large litter. Talk to friends or club members and, if possible, borrow items from them. You may need premature feeding bottles but these may be difficult to find. If you can borrow them, all the better. The chances are, if you are prepared for any eventuality, all will go well.

CARING FOR THE BITCH

The vet will have examined your bitch and all appears well. Spread her food over the day, three or four meals are better than one big meal. If it is a big litter, her stomach may already be distended, without a huge intake of food. If you already feed a complete diet, follow the manufacturer's diet sheets for in-whelp bitches. If you feed ox-tripe etc. seek your vet's advice about supplements. Always have plenty of clean water available. Feed your bitch as well as you can if you want to have a healthy litter. Do not fall into the trap of thinking that a double dose of calcium or vitamins will provide the unborn puppies with good strong bone. It will not; it may cause untold damage to the puppies. Trust your vet, or fellow breeders who have produced good stock, for advice.

The bitch will still need exercise; two or three short walks on the lead will suffice. Do not force her to go if she is reluctant. If she appears to be uncomfortable, check the arm-pits and the area between the hind legs as she may have developed small reddened, patches due to friction. Spread the area with mild antiseptic cream. Check daily for any signs of distress or discharge. If the discharge is clear, all is usually well. If it is dark or bloody have your vet examine her. Depending on the size of the litter you may see movement of the puppies when the bitch lies on her side. This is always a welcome sign. The average period of gestation is 63 days, so everyone assumes that the puppies will be whelped 63 days after the mating takes place. Be prepared! We have had a litter as early as 57 days after mating and another as late as 70 days after mating. There were only three puppies in the latter. Watch the bitch carefully after the 56th day. If she goes off her food or develops a discharge, take her temperature. The normal temperature should be 100-100.5 degrees Fahrenheit or 37.7-38 degrees Centigrade. If there is a distinct rise or fall, consult your vet. If all is going well, there should be a drop in temperature 24 to 48 hours before whelping is due to commence. It may drop to 98°F or 36.6°C. This is only a general guide.

THE WHELPING

By this time you will have introduced the bitch to her whelping quarters. She may begin to 'prepare' her bed by scratching up the newspapers etc. The vulva may appear much larger and very floppy. When there is a watery discharge, this is telling you that whelping is due to commence. The bitch may become restless; she may begin to pant. She will begin to strain and may look towards her hindquarters. If all is well, she will give a huge push and a puppy will emerge from the vulva. It may come feet first or head first; it may still be in its sac or the sac may have burst. *Do not panic*. In most cases, the puppy drops into the whelping box and the bitch immediately commences to clean it up. The after-birth or placenta is attached to the puppy by a long umbilical cord. The bitch will eat the placenta and sever the cord with her teeth.

If the puppy does not come away with the first push, get a piece of sterile gauze and hold the puppy gently but firmly until the bitch pushes again. *Do not pull.* The second or third push usually expels the puppy. If the puppy does not come away, seek help immediately. The length of time between the birth of a succession of puppies varies considerably. It may be anything between ten minutes to half and hour or more. If the bitch is relaxed and caring for the puppy/puppies already born, there is no cause for alarm. See that each puppy is placed on a teat and is able to suckle. If the whelping is fairly rapid and there are many puppies, you can put them into the specially prepared cardboard boxes. As long as the puppies seem content they can be left in the box for half-an-hour or so. They can be returned to the bitch during a lull in the whelping programme. Some bitches are very possessive and resent any interference. You should know your bitch and you must use your discretion. Ensure that the hot-water bottles are completely covered by the pieces of blanket. If time permits between births, you can check for deformities – crank tails, hare lips and cleft palates. Hare lips are easy to see, as the lip is split up to the nostrils. Cleft palates are not so easy for the layman to diagnose. Sometimes it is easy to see – when the puppy suckles, the milk oozes out of the nostrils. A puppy who is fairly large and strong can be encouraged to suck on your little finger. Turn your finger gently, until you can feel the roof of the mouth. This way you can feel if the palate is entire. If you find you have any deformed puppies and prefer that the vet disposes of them, please keep them warm in a cardboard box until you can hand them over. The incidence of deformities is variable. A repeat mating can give totally different results. One litter may produce puppies with defects, while the other litter may produce a uniform set of puppies with no visible defects.

It is advisable to keep records of the time of each birth, the weight of each puppy and the distinguishing colours or deformities. At the same time you should be able to tell the sex of each puppy. It is vital to count the number of placentas/afterbirths expelled. Eating the placentas is natural for the bitch and each puppy has its own one. If the sac bursts before the puppy has been whelped, the placenta is retained and this could cause complications – hence the need to check carefully and to keep the vet informed about any discrepancies. Occasionally a puppy may be born with the membrane or sac intact. In this case, break the sac immediately so that the puppy can breathe. Listen to the puppies and if they begin to make a squealing noise rather like seagulls, it may be an indication that all is not well. A healthy, contented puppy will make very little noise except for an occasional squeal. If there is a constant, high-pitched squeal, it is an indication that all is not well and you must inform the vet immediately.

Many novice breeders are worried when they see the newborn puppies, as many of them have pink noses and feet. The colour may also cause alarm, as even the fawns are covered in dark hairs. Most of these hairs disappear as the puppies grow and the noses and feet turn black. The ears are very small and are usually laid flat against the head. The black muzzles are there at birth. If not, there is little chance that they will appear later. Slight white areas on the bottom lip and the toes may disappear after a few days. Large areas of white may grow larger with the puppy. They are easier to see on brindles. Some puppies may have excess black on the chest, the tail and down the backs of the legs. This may or may not disappear. This is where a knowledge of the bloodlines will help. If any of the puppies appear lifeless, clear the mouth of mucus and rub gently, but firmly with a rough piece of towelling. In many cases this will invigorate the puppy. Additionally, if the flesh around the nose and lips is blue, or pale grey, it is safe to assume that the puppy is dead.

AFTER THE BIRTH

When the bitch seems fully relaxed and she has ceased straining, try to persuade her to go outside. Sometimes this is easier said than done, as many bitches are loath to leave their puppies. If she will go out, this gives you a chance to tidy up the whelping box and to put in the hygienic bedding. When the bitch returns, give her a warm drink to which a little glucose has been added. Settle her in the box and return all the healthy puppies to her. The majority of puppies seem to make an appearance in the small hours of the morning. When it is surgery time, call your vet. If the bitch does not relax, if she continues to strain and does not produce another puppy, ring for the vet immediately. If you have a good relationship with your vet, he or she will come out. If not, you may have to take the bitch into the surgery. Do not hesitate. The delay in seeking help may mean death for the bitch, the puppy or both. The vet may need to perform a caesarean section, but if action is taken early enough, there should not be any complications.

Normally, the milk will appear as the puppies are born. Each puppy must be put on a teat as soon as possible, so that it can get some of the colostrum which abounds in the early supply of milk. This gets the puppy off to a good start and nothing can replace it. Sometimes the bitch does not have a supply of milk. In some cases the vet will give her an injection which will induce the flow of milk. If this does not work, you may be able to provide a foster mother, or resort to bottle-feeding. If you have made careful preparations, you will have laid in a supply of puppy milk, bottles etc. Take care that the milk is not too hot and the hole in the teat is not too large. If you have to resort to bottle-feeding you must give a small amount every two hours, round the clock. Wipe the surplus off the mouth after every puppy has been fed. With luck, the bitch may lick each puppy, thus activating normal bowel and bladder functions. If she will not do this, use a piece of sterile lint or gauze moistened with warm water, and gently massage around the anus, the penis and the vulva. This will activate the puppy's internal workings and it must be done after every meal. Or you can massage the puppy with your finger, as I suggest in the next chapter when referring to orphaned puppies.

Watch the bitch carefully for any signs of aggression towards the puppies. Most bitches make good mothers *but*, as in the human race, some hate their offspring. If the bitch growls or snaps at her puppies, it may be advisable to muzzle her while she feeds them – always assuming that she has milk. If the puppies can feed from her, all the better; but it would not be wise to ask the bitch to clean the puppies. You must do this, as you would if you were bottle-feeding them.

So, the last puppy has been whelped and the bitch has been examined by the vet. What now?

THE FIRST TWO WEEKS
The main considerations are to ensure that the puppies are kept warm, dry, clean and quiet. If you have an infra-red lamp fixed over the whelping box, fix it over one end, rather than in the centre. This will give the bitch a chance to move away from the heat while the puppies can be underneath the lamp. Many puppies die because of loss of body heat. If they are content, they lie together making little noise other than contented squeals. If they have been fed, they will spread out under the heat. If they are cold they will try to huddle close together and they become restless. Watch out for this and listen to the sounds they make. You will learn to recognise the difference between the sounds of contentment and the sounds of distress.

For the first few days after whelping there may be a dark-coloured discharge from the bitch, so it is essential to change the bedding two or three times each day. The modern veterinary bedding can be put in the washing machine and it dries quickly. If you are not using this, try to cover the bottom of the whelping box with layers of clean newsprint or brown paper. This can be disposed of in an incinerator. If the box is kept clean, it will also be dry. If you have small children, do not allow them to disturb the bitch and her puppies during the early days. Some bitches are very protective of their puppies and may resent interference. They may even crush the puppies in an endeavour to protect them. They may "snap" at those who they think are unwelcome visitors.

If the milk supply from the bitch is adequate, the puppies will appear to grow before your eyes. Most puppies are quite dark in colour when they are born, but as they develop, the coats become lighter. Some people have imagined that puppies were brindle because of the darkness of their coats. Quite often, the nose, the lips, and the pads on the feet are pink or grey in colour, but they usually go black as the puppies develop. A good, contented, bitch will clean her puppies regularly, thus activating their bowels and bladders. If it is a big litter, the odd puppy may be overlooked. Check from time to time, and if necessary, clean the undersides of the tails with a moist piece of gauze. Check the bitch's teats. If they are hard, or red and swollen, seek help from the vet immediately, as the bitch may develop mastitis.

If the litter is small and there is a good supply of milk, the puppies will grow a little quicker. Check their claws to see that they are short. If they are long, cut off the points, or their pumping action will scratch the bitch's teats. A good mother is loath to leave her puppies, but you must get her outside from time to time. This will give you a chance to clean the whelping box and to examine each puppy. See that she has an adequate supply of clean drinking water at all times. The water helps the milk supply. If the puppies sound happy and contented, do not attempt to introduce extra milk. This often causes more problems than people imagine, as the small stomachs are unable to deal with the extra supply. Feed the bitch as well as you can and she will turn the good food and clean drinking water into good milk. As the puppies reach nine or ten days of age, you will notice that the eyes are beginning to open. There may be a slight trace of mucus and this can be bathed away with clean gauze and sterile water. If the eyelids are swollen and there is a lot of mucus, ask the vet to examine the puppy, or puppies, concerned. It may be a minor infection, or it may be the onset of entropion. Prompt treatment may ward off serious problems later. The "pig rail", which was secured in the whelping box at the onset of whelping, will be removed when the bitch begins to resent it. She may begin to chew it. This is why the area inside the "pig rail" was made big, so that the bitch could lie down in comfort and the tiny puppies behind her back would be pushed out of harm's way. As the puppies grow bigger, their squeals grow louder and if you are within earshot you can hear them, before they are suffocated. Round-the-clock vigilance is essential for the first two weeks, and longer still, if you can manage it. Check the puppies daily for any abnormality. The coats should be sleek and shiny. The remnants of the umbilical chords will shrivel up and drop off. *Do not pull them off*, as this may cause a sore place or a hernia. The puppies should look good; they should sound happy and contented; they should smell sweet.

ORPHAN PUPPIES

From time to time, as I have said, nature lets us down and, despite injections from the vet, there is no milk. It is sometimes possible to find a bitch who has only one or two puppies, and she may take to the extra family. I have known bitches who loved rearing puppies and would take in an extra family as soon as their own puppies were taken away. Time is essential. Ask around so that help is at hand as quickly as possible. However, you may have the sad event of losing not only the bitch's milk but the bitch herself, and being unable to find a foster mother, so provision must be made for rearing the puppies by hand. If you have become a member of a breed club or a canine society, you will doubtless know of someone who has the miniature feeding bottles I mentioned. There are various milk substitutes on the market and you must obey the maker's instructions to the letter. See that all the equipment is sterile and do not skimp on the night-time feeds. At the beginning you must be prepared to bottle feed every two hours, round the clock. This can later be reduced to three hours. Regular meal times are essential if you are to rear the puppies.

Have two cardboard boxes on hand, each containing a covered hot-water bottle. Put all the puppies into one of the boxes. Each puppy, in turn, must be fed and cleaned up – yes, your finger must take up the duties of a bitch's tongue. A little Vaseline on it will help. With your finger, use a gentle stroking motion on the puppy, who will then do the necessary, emptying both the bowels and the bladder. When you are satisfied, the puppy should be dried and put in the other box, for the puppies which have been fed. This way there is no chance of one puppy being fed twice and one missing out altogether. When all the puppies are fed, clean up the whelping box and return the puppies.

THE DEVELOPING LITTER

The eyes should now be opened and they should be blue. If they are opaque or cloudy, consult your vet. The darker the blue of the eyes, the darker the mature eyes should be. The deciduous, or "milk" teeth, begin to erupt from three to four weeks. These are usually very sharp and you may notice that the bitch may tend to wince as the puppies suckle. Some bitches may refuse to lie down and you may find the puppies sitting on their hindquarters and attempting to suckle from this position. The puppies are now beginning to move on all fours, instead of propelling themselves around by the forelegs. Watch carefully and take note of any puppy whose movement is suspect. In the first few days, movement will be very erratic – two steps forward and five steps back. As they try to face up to each other, they may wobble from side to side. This is natural. Your concern will be the puppy who does not seem able to get up on all four legs. If you spot one like that, seek advice at once.

WEANING

From about three weeks you can introduce weaning, especially if it is a big litter. If you use a complete diet for your adults you will doubtless wish to do the same for your puppies. Again, follow the instructions carefully. The people who have compiled these diets have studied for years the nutritional value of the food content – the vitamins, minerals etc. If you find one which suits your puppies, stick to it. Do not chop and change, as this will play havoc with the digestive system. I must be honest in stating that we are lucky (or maybe "old-fashioned", depending on your point of view) in that we have always reared our litters on natural foods. Some meat, with the bulk of the fat removed, can be frozen in small blocks. This makes it easy to grate the meat on a nutmeg grater. Feed when thawed out. The first introduction is a portion about the size of a pea,

Weaning can be a messy business to begin with, but it is not long before the puppies get the idea.

By seven weeks of age the puppies will be fully weaned, and it will be time to start looking for new homes.

placed on the end of a finger. I have never known it to fail. Try this twice per day and make sure every puppy gets a fair share. After a few days each portion can be a little larger. Any supplements can be added to the food, but care must be taken that you do not give extra supplements to try and build better bone. Too much can cause far more damage than too little. If you trust your vet, ask for advice. Worm treatment can be administered this way also.

Around this time the puppies should be beginning to see and hear. Tap gently on the side of the whelping box and they should turn their heads in the direction of the noise. When you have gained their attention, move your finger slowly from side to side. The puppies will move their heads from side to side. Beware, the puppies might attempt to bite, and milk teeth, as I have said, can be very sharp. By this time the bitch may have decided that she needs more time to herself. If she is within earshot of the litter, she will rush in if she senses danger. There is no hard and fast rule as to when you take the puppies away from their dam, or vice-versa. Some are so attached to their offspring that you have almost to drag them away. Others are glad to sneak away when the puppies are two weeks old. With the latter, have patience. As long as she feeds them regularly, cleans them well and stays with them overnight, do not force her to stay with them the rest of the time.

Once the puppies have begun to accept solid food, it should be easy to wean them completely. The meals should be regular, and care must be taken to see that each puppy gets a fair share. It is easier to put all the food into one big bowl, but it is not wise. A greedy puppy will eat until sick, while a slower one may fail to develop. Six small meals per day are better than three large ones for the puppies, if not for you. As the puppies grow, the number of meals can be reduced and the content increased. Clean drinking water must always be available. In recent years it has been declared that cow's milk and raw eggs are bad for the dogs. We have gone from grated ox-cheek, to cubed ox-cheek. We also feed cow's tripe, raw. We have never used sheep's paunches because of the risk of tape worms. Cow's hearts and kidneys can be cooked and so can liver. We have never fed biscuit meal with meat, tripe or offal. Hard biscuits are fed separately. Scrambled or boiled eggs with cheese provides a nourishing treat. Cooked fish with the bones carefully removed is another tasty meal. Puppies do appreciate variety. Remove any left-over food after each meal.

It is over thirty years since our first vet said: "A good coat goes in at the mouth. A dog who is fed well, with good food, should develop into a strong, healthy animal with a loose skin, topped by a shiny coat. The bones will be strong and the eyes will be bright." However you feed your puppies, you must give the new owners advance notice and complete diet sheets. This will enable them to lay in a stock of food, or find local suppliers. If for any reason they have to change the diet, it must be done as slowly as possible to avoid any distress or, worse still, stomach upsets.

Chapter Nine

THE BULLMASTIFF IN THE UK

IN THE BEGINNING

For most people the early years were dominated by the name Farcroft, which I have discussed in Chapter One. I must confess that I, too, once thought that this name was the keyword for Bullmastiffs. For a period of time litters were bred for which Mrs Moseley was registered as the breeder. Some of the ancestors were down as Farcroft, others as Hamil or of the Hamil. Then, many years ago, I had a letter from an elderly gentleman who said that both were the names of places where S. E. Moseley had lived. In October 1925 a complaint was made against Moseley for false representation of a photograph. There had already been a complaint about a dog registered as Farcroft Formidable – a registration which was later cancelled. The UK *Kennel Gazette* carried the following information: "In reference to the pedigree complaints, the Secretary placed before the Committee discrepancies in the date of birth and pedigrees of various dogs."

Another name which comes to mind is that of Mr J. Barrowcliffe, who had the Parkvale affix and, if I am correct, he had Mastiffs with the Stapleford affix; but these were unregistered. It was obvious that there was a lot of rivalry and ill-feeling between the two men, and Moseley accused Barrowcliffe of breeding Bullmastiffs which were really poor Mastiffs.

There were also two Ramsdens; whether they were brothers or otherwise, I know not. The earlier one was Bob Ramsden, and the slightly later one H. E. Ramsden. Bob Ramsden bred Captain, whose name was changed to Tiger of Silverglen, and Derby Countess, whose name was changed to Bessie of Silverglen. Silverglen was the affix of Mr L. Prestidge. I am indebted to Mr Prestidge's son for the pedigrees and photographs of his father's dog and bitch. He also gave me a newspaper clipping, dated November 5th 1927, which reads: "I should imagine the youngest fancier in Derbyshire at the present time is little Miss Jose Howe. In any case she will be the youngest Bullmastiff breeder. Jose has a lot of toys and on her last birthday decided to have a dog instead. A visit to Mr Prestidge, Normanton Road, Derby, resulted in the purchase of one of his Silverglen strain of Bullmastiffs, a very smart fawn bitch, with a black mask. This bitch is named Sheila and she is a good all-round specimen of the Bullmastiff – and so she ought to be, seeing her sire is Tiger of Silverglen and her mother Bessie of Silverglen, both having won many prizes, and both being holders of challenge cups. Sheila, when old enough, was mated to Jumbo of Stapleford, a fawn dog owned by Mr Hird; his parents are Tiger Torus and Juno, so Bullmastiff blood of the best is to be found in the litter Sheila has presented. There are six in the litter; three are fawn and three are brindle and all of them possess the coveted black mask. Miss Howe has a very large kennel for them, with a large wired-in run for exercising. Although so young – Miss Howe is only six years of age – she takes a great deal of interest in her dogs. Of course, her mother, Mrs Howe, sees to the feeding department etc."

ABOVE: One of Vic Smith's earliest bitches – thought to be the dam of Tiger Prince.

LEFT: Mr L. Prestidge pictured with Bessie of Silverglen.

A brindle bitch, Farcroft Silvo, was the first breed Champion. She was registered in August 1925. Her sire and dam, Hamil Grip and Farcroft Belltong, were not registered until August 1927, and there the trail ends. Tiger Prince, a red-fawn, was the second Champion and the first dog. He was registered in December 1925 (Tiger Torus–Princess Poppy). Tiger Torus was by Farcroft Fidelity ex Farcroft Storm (Unr). Princess Poppy was by Stapleford Brutus (Brutus of Parkvale on some pedigrees) ex Borrace.

BULL-MASTIFFS (PURE-BRED)
It was not until October 1927 that the Bull-Mastiffs (Pure-Bred) were included in the Register of Breeds. This contained 16 registrations (one later cancelled) and the photographs of Dileas and Ruby of Ranald. Ruby of Ranald was originally registered as Farcroft Tracker. Many owners and breeders did not have an affix and this made pedigree research difficult. Between 1925 and 1937 there were over sixty Princesses – Princess Betty, Princess Judy etc. If a puppy was brindle in colour, this came into the name – Brindle Bob, Brindle Betty etc. Tiger was also very popular – Tiger Superb, Tiger's Double etc.

As the breed became more popular, genuine breeders began to register their kennel name or affix. Some have become quite famous and others have faded into oblivion. E. Burton's Navigation first appeared in 1927, just before Vic Smith's Pridzor. One of the most famous was 'of the Fenns', the affix of J. E. V. Toney. In August 1930 there were two registrations: Poppy of the

Bepagain of Bulmas and Binagain of Bulmas: Both were exported to the USA, where they became Champions.

Fenns, bitch, Mr J. E. V. Toney; (Don Juan–Tiger Princess) bred by Mr G. F. Wedgwood; whelped September 10th 1929; and Roger of the Fenns, dog, Mr J. E. V. Toney; (Don Juan–Luzlow Princess) bred by Mr G. F. Wedgwood; whelped November 7th 1929. Roger was to become a Champion and was one of only two dogs to sire ten Champions, the other being Ch. Billy of Stanfell, dog, Mr J. Higginson; (Springwell Simba Ch.–Bessie of Stanfell) bred by owner; whelped July 14th 1943. It is hardly surprising to note that Roger was the paternal grandsire of Billy and one of the maternal great-grandsires. September 1930 saw the first Bulmas registration – Sheila of Bulmas, bitch, Mrs G. E. Hill and Mr C. R. Leeke; (Rusty Rufus–Tara) bred by Mr S. Pattisch; whelped July 20th 1929. Sheila was to become the foundation bitch of the world-renowned Bulmas Kennels.

In the early years, breeders and exhibitors came from all walks of life. HRH the Duke of Gloucester had a dog named Hussar Stingo; the Hon. Mrs J. Murray-Smith bred and owned Athos, who won his first CC at the breed's second Championship show in Manchester 1928; Ch. Jeanie of Wynyard was bred by the Marquis of Londonderry and owned by the Hon. Mrs J. Murray-Smith; and Gordon Richards, the Champion jockey, so loved the breed that he gave a trophy to the Southern Bullmastiff Society. Film stars, authors, footballers all became owners of Bullmastiffs. Eric Makins, writing for *The American Bullmastiff*, stated that, when Her Majesty the Queen and Her Royal Highness Princess Margaret were very small children, they had a Bullmastiff puppy, but I cannot vouch for that. There are so many names of historical interest that it makes it difficult to decide where to draw the line. Early 1934 saw the first mention of Stanfell, followed later by Springwell. In January 1935 Jeanette of Brooklands, bred by Mr T. Pennington, was registered. She was exported to Mr John W. Cross Jnr of the US. She became a US Ch. but, when John Cross fell ill, she came back to the UK and became a UK Ch. but, sad to say, the KCSB does not make any mention of her US title.

September 1935 marked a turning point for brindles when Mrs F. A. M. Warren registered the first 'of Harbex' litter – six dogs and two bitches. Amongst them was Big Bill of Harbex, registered as a sable golden brindle. Big Bill must be behind all the brindles alive today. Thinking of brindles, I find it hard to understand why they fell out of favour. The second brindle Champion

Ch. Beauty of Stanfell, whelped 1941.

Ch. Wisdom of Wynyard.

Pearly King of Harbex (right) and Peregrine of Harbex.

Tawny Lion: Height at shoulder 29 ins, weight approx. 11 stone, bred by Mrs O. Shelley, whelped 1945.

Barnswood Gamekeeper (Stocktonian Artificer – Barnswood Enchantress), whelped 1946.

was a bitch, Silbrin, and she was the twenty-first Champion in the breed's history. Chips of Harbex, a dog and a great-great-grandson of Big Bill of Harbex, became the third brindle Champion, but only the seventy-first Champion in the breed's history. He was registered as a golden tiger brindle. Up to the outbreak of the Second World War 40 Champions were made up, 24 dogs and 16 bitches, two of them brindle. The bitch CCs were withheld at the SKC Edinburgh, and the Crystal Palace in London in 1938 and Bath in 1938. The last pre-war Championship show was held in Harrogate in September 1939. Dog shows with CCs on offer for our breed were not held again until 1946. Until then, many affixes had made their place in the KCSB. Alongside those

Ch. Bruce of Radcot (Ch. Billy of Stanfell – Radcot Enterprise), bred by Mrs and Mrs Clark, whelped 1949.

already mentioned came Arpens, Bartonville, Bowdencourt, Bridewell, Castlehill, Cockfosters, Conheath, Fenchurch, Kenwood, le Tasyll, Mackwyn, Maritime, Millbrook, Navigation, Nunsoe, Rhyolite, Rodenhurst, Rosland, Sealton, Valdor, Woolowin and Westgate. Mention· must be made of those who kept the breed going during the difficult war years – Bartica, Bulmas, Bulwyn, Barnswood, Carrokid, Chestonian, of the Fenns, Ferox, Gracedieu, Goodyear, Harbex, Hickathrift, Harecastle, Jayessem, le Tasyll, Lyndorgar, Kennerleigh, Kingstone, Mabenly, Maeben, Maritime, Moonday, Mulorna, Navigation, Pyntyrch, Pridzor, Stanfell, Stocktonian, Taffside, Thorneyside, Rosland, and Rosland combined with le Tasyll, Valdor, and Wilmcourt. Without these the breed may have died out. If I have omitted any of the breeders and affixes of the formative years, I am sorry – but is not easy to compress the story of the Bullmastiff into one volume!

POST-WAR
In the late 1940s Bablock, Lisvane, and the original Marbette came on the scene. The first Buttonoak was registered in 1949, closely followed by Tipdixon, Bullturn, Goodstock, Bulstaff and Swatchway. 1952 saw Ellisdene and in 1955 came the first Wyaston litter. 1956 saw Tipdixon, Ivywill and the original Maybrook. In 1957 there were Gimingham and Lingmell, followed in 1958 by Oldwell, Yorkist and Copperfield, and Kelwall in 1959. As with every breed, people breed one or two litters and then they just disappear. In the 1960s there were Bulmead, Doubleforte, Deerhaddon, Walkmyll, Vorsodene – none of them now in existence. Lombardy came in then, and is still with us. 1961 gave us St Mungo, which is in many of today's litters, because of one bitch, St Mungo Minerva, bred by Joy Watkins. In 1962 Joyce James came in with the Morejoy affix and, in the same year, Dorothy Butler bred one litter in which there were two dogs and two bitches. One dog went to Harry Collias, where he became Ch. Oldwell Toby of Studbergh. He sired nine Champions and in my opinion he was an excellent dog.

In 1963 a combination of Goodstock and Tipdixon gave us the basis of the Naukeen Kennels,

*ABOVE: Ch. Pridzor's Trust (Ch.
Billy of Standfell – Radcot
Enterprise) whelped 1950.*

*RIGHT: Harry Colliass with Ch.
Bambino (Ace of Buttonoak –
Mayqueen of Marbette): The first
Oldwell Champion, whelped 1957.*

which are still going strong today. In 1964 there was also a very good litter bred by Ken and
Maureen Gaulton, from which came the Champions Taurus and Triumph Herald of Mureken. Mrs
Parkes came in with the Silverfarm affix. Silverfarm was renowned for the temperament of the
stock produced and many of the dogs were brindles. Barbara Browning's Barloy affix and Mollie
Elliott's Ellney affix were there in June 1965 and July saw the registration of our first Champion,
Darrell of Kelwall, and Joyce James' first Champion, Morejoy Eastern Princess. Names which
came in with litters registered in 1966 were Tyffynon, Kirkleatham, Woodhaven, Lynriver,
Gillipenny, Garamond, Sandene and Saxstead, followed in 1967 by Bullpug, Vaward, Securus,
Overdeben, Showell, Freefarm and Franbar. 1968 saw the registration of the first Graecia litter.
And there was an Edialhouse litter late that year. In 1969 Bill Toogood had a litter, which was
registered as Wickham but later bore the affix Wickaven. Mrs Marsh came on the scene with
Marmoss, followed by Mr and Mrs C. Woods with Clywoods. By the end of 1969 the number of
Champions had risen to 167 – 90 dogs and 77 bitches.
    1970 saw Miss Chamberlain's Ladydale affix, and the registration of one of the best bitches I
have ever seen, Ch. Pekingtown Abece, bred by the late John Coles. Alas, there is no decent

Ch. Wyaston Tudor Prince (Wyaston Captain Cuttle – Wyaston Tudor Lass), bred by D.B. Oliff, owned by Dr J. Clark.

Ch. Little Miss of Oldwell (Sh. Ch. Toby of Studbergh – Ch. Miss Oldwell): Crufts Best of Breed, bred and owned by Harry Colliass.

pictorial record of her. Jim and Ethel Leeson checked in with their first litter and the first name was Pitmans Gentleman Jim. Dennis and Jean Alder came in with Simbec, and Sid Ford and his wife with Tamanu. This also marked the period when the KC added the affix Index to any puppies registered without affix. There was new blood with Tuachair, Masterdon, Broadbeam, Shebrynn, Boeton, Coombelane, Jonjersi, Tryndehayes and Salvateo. Most of these affixes are now occasional names on some pedigrees, but some went on to make a name for themselves. Coombelane Ideal Partner was the first Bullmastiff to be featured in a TV covering of Crufts. How well I remember the late Stanley Dangerfield describing him to all the viewers!

1971 saw an upsurge of interest in Scotland, when Kathleen Pettigrew registered Damaron Admiration and Damaron Aristo Gold. It was the year in which we bred our first Scottish Champion, Frederick of Kelwall. In England, Harry Colliass bred a litter by Ch. Regent of Oldwell ex Ch. Oldwell Queen Gwenevive of Mureken and from this litter came Maverick of Oldwell. Maverick was sold to Gerald and Doris Warren. Over the years he has appeared on pedigrees as Copperfield Maverick of Oldwell, Maverick of Oldwell of Copperfield and Maverick of Copperfield of Oldwell, but all these names belong to the same dog. By the end of 1971 there had

TOP LEFT: Ch. Morejoy Eastern Princess (Gimingham Checkmate – Morejoy Captains Lady), bred and owned by Mrs J. James.

ABOVE: Ch. Darrell of Kelwall (Ch. Oldwell Toby of Studbergh – Cortella of Kelwall): The first Kelwall Champion, bred and owned by Lyn and Walter Pratt.

LEFT: Ch. Showell Zarbor (Ch. Oldwell Toby of Studbergh – Cortessa of Kelwall), bred and owned by Don and Brenda Cook.

Photo: Diane Pearce.

been 174 Champions in the breed. The name Beau Delachase appeared in 1972. This dog won two CCs in the same week, but the name does not appear in the show ring now. There was also Bullborough Bulmir and Terarn. In March Janet McKnight bred a litter of which one became a Champion, Knightguard Black Douglas. His litter brother, Knightguard Macgregor, was exported to New Zealand where he had great influence on the breed. Later in the year Mr Cato appeared with the Recnad affix. June saw the first appearance of Bill and Fran Harris' Bunsoro affix; also Viclaydell, Cherholme, Seacross, Cravenhouse, Leontas and Suttonoak.

1973 saw the first of the Lucas' Doomwatch litters. It also saw the first of the Lowries' litters, one puppy of which went to Crawford Taylor, who later started the Bryany Bullmastiffs. By this time the KC had changed the Index affix and was using Kenstaff. Oldebill and St Mungo came in April, and Twynfields in May. Another short-lived affix was Tayvallich, whose owner died suddenly. In April of 1973 we had a litter of puppies by Azer of Oldwell ex Ailsa of Kelwall. We retained a brindle bitch puppy, Bonnie of Kelwall, and although we did not realise it at the time, she was destined to be the first brindle Champion for twenty-five years, and only the fourth in the breed's history. The Lowries bred their first litter with an affix in 1974 and they used Learigg.

ABOVE: Ch. Pitmans Gentleman Jim (Bulstaff Turvey – Lady Cleopatra of Naukeen), bred and owned by Jim and Ethel Leeson.

TOP RIGHT: Ch. Yorkist Miss Muffet (Salvateo Don Sebastian of Jensymon – Yorkist Miss Meryl), bred and owned by Margaret Reynolds.

CENTRE RIGHT: Ch. Doomwatch Gipsy Oldwell (Azer of Oldwell – Ch. Yorkist Maid Marion): Top winning Bulmastiff bitch in 1974, bred by J. & B. Lucas, owned by Harry Colliass.

BOTTOM RIGHT: Ch. Colom Florin (Ch. Lombardy Simon of Silverfarm– Lombardy Rosamunda), bred and owned by Mary Cox.

However, it transpired that the affix was already in use, so it was changed to the more familiar Leyrigg. The all-rounder Mr G. Down came into the breed and registered a litter with the Weycombe affix. The Campbells registered their first litter with the affix Clyth, and Jean Clarke followed in November, with Kwintra. Colom came in at the end of the year. January 1975 saw a litter registered by Bill and Jan Newton under the affix Craigylea. I doubt if anyone reading this has not heard about Ch. Craigylea Sir Galahad. Two affixes which were short-lived were Maedeen and Marchfield. Petabrook also appeared but it stayed around for some time. Three litters carrying the Gadrian affix were registered by Mr and Mrs Butler. The Marbette affix had lain dormant for many years but it was resurrected in October 1975, though to date it has not gained any of its former glory. By the end of 1975 there were 194 Champions, 106 dogs and 88 bitches.

THE LAST TWENTY YEARS
As far as breed records go, 1976 was a year of importance.
On July 24th at the British Bullmastiff League Championship Show, Granville Blount awarded Bonnie of Kelwall her third CC and BOB. This meant that after twenty-five years there was a brindle Champion – the second home-bred and the third bitch. The other brindle was a dog. On the same day that Bonnie became a Champion, a special litter was whelped. The breeders were Dr and Mrs J.E.B. Fraser; the sire was Ch. Nicholas of Oldwell and the dam was St Mungo Minerva. In that litter there were four puppies destined to make history. Frazer, Kracka, Verona and Yoric of Oldwell all became Champions. Prior to this, Champions Mi Beauty, Mi Dinah and Mi Hope of Marbette, whelped on the 4th of September 1956, held the record, being three Champions from

Ch. Bunsoro Bombadier (Ch. Bombadillo of Bunsoro – Ch. Bunsoro Dianna), bred and owned by Bill and Fran Harris.

Ch. Barloy Nice One (Ch. Mystic of Oldwell – Barloy Hebreena), bred and owned by Barbara Browning.

ABOVE: Ch. Todomas Tamar (Ch. Bunsoro Bombadier – Delilah of Bunsoro), bred and owned by Tom Massey.

TOP RIGHT: Ch. Twynfields Bryden (Twynfields Sampson – Twynfields Bonny Belinda), bred and owned by Phil and Margaret Calverley.

RIGHT: Ch. Dreadnot Melody Maker (Hrothgar of Tartuffe – Ch. Naukeen Melody Maker), bred and owned by Margaret McNaught.

one litter. During 1976 Copperfield Ben Allen shone, winning BIS at more than one Open Show. Bunsoro Dianna repeated her success of the previous year by going BIS at Nidderdale Open Show. Craigylea Sir Galahad was BIS at British Timkin Open Show. Names which would make their marks in later years were registered in Eastlynn and Bryany litters.

Dennis Newton's Pitmans Drummer Boy took over the following year when he won a trophy which had been donated for the Bullmastiff winning the most points in Open Shows. Copperfield Ben Allen, now a Champion, also managed a few more BIS wins. Ch. Craigylea Sir Galahad won the Working Group at Crufts. In 1978 Crufts was staged at Olympia, London for the last time. The Bullmastiff Society of Scotland held their first Championship Show and Beryl Collins was the judge. Frank Pesticcio made the journey to the show from his home in Wales. It was his seventieth birthday. Bunsoro Jimson made his debut in a television film made about the Brontes and Haworth Vicarage. Kracka of Oldwell won his first CC and was winner of the Working Group at the SKC.

Ch. Maxstoke Elkie (Ch. Bold Borage Jagofpeeko – Maxstoke Cleopatra), bred and owned by Colin and Mary Jones.

Ch. Jagofpeeko Wood Sorrel (Ch. Maxstoke Boldherbie Jagofpeeko – Ch. Jaghofpeeko Boadicea), bred and owned by Ewart Grant.

In 1979 Bullmastiffs were one of three large breeds in the Working Group at Crufts which had poor classifications – no puppy or junior classes, just Special Yearling, which was very hard on the younger stock. The world-famous D.J. (Dorothea Daniell Jenkins) expressed regret that many good dogs of the smaller type were being passed over for larger dogs which were more like Mastiffs. While I was in Canada, I made a trip to the US and I saw Ch. Ironwoods Prince of Darkness, who many said was black. In fact, he was a very good, very dark, brindle.

Frederick of Kelwall, who had a Working Group at the Border Union Championship Show to his credit, won BIS at Falkirk Open Show under the late Harry Glover. In his critique Harry wrote: "A Bullmastiff and a show stealer ..... If there was one point which persuaded me to give him BIS it was his movement. I have never seen better in the breed."

1980 and Crufts was still in London at Earls Court. There were five classes for each sex: Novice, Special Yearling, Post Graduate, Limit and Open, which did not give much scope for the younger animals. Christopher Habig came over in summer to judge the Welsh and West of England's Open Show, and he said that he was surprised at the wide variation in type and size. He claimed that the breed was more uniform in Germany. In the same year, the Breed Council were to consider an interpretation of movement for inclusion in the Breed Standard.

Crufts 1981 saw the same number of classes, but Special Yearling was now replaced by Special Junior. Beryl Collins judged the breed and her final decision rested on father and daughter – Ch. Bombadillo of Bunsoro and Bunsoro Proud Mary. At Blackpool Harry Colliass made Ch. Colom Jumbo BOB, who went on to win the Working Group under Violet Yates. Looking back on the

Ch. Movern Elyse (Bronson of Bunsoro at Todomas – Morvern Dulcie), bred and owned by Malcolm and Angela McInnes.

Photo: John Hartley.

Ch. Eastlynn Victoria to Taurleone (Ch. Boomerang of Naukeen – Naukeen Ballad to Eastlynn), bred by Marie Qualters, owned by Mrs O. Fowler.

Ch. Bournevalley Misty at Meitza (Bournevalley's Conan – Bournevalley's Freya), bred by Anne and Duncan Bowman, owned by Marie Landers and Fiona Miller.

*Ch. Licassa Jolly
Roger (Ch. Oldwell
Saint – Licassa Lady
Rogina), bred and
owned by Barry
Blunden and Chris
Quantrill.*

Blackpool Championship Shows, Harry Colliass judged the breed there in 1967 and he made Darrell of Kelwall BOB. Darrell went on to win the Working Group and the Reserve BIS under the late Viscount Chelmsford. No Bullmastiff has achieved Reserve BIS at a Championship Show since that date. By this time there were more than 200 Champions in the breed and seven of them were brindles. Names which would come up in later years in top classes were Cadenham, Tartuffe and Wyburn.

Crufts 1982 had five classes for each sex and there were 23 Championship shows throughout the year, nine of which were held between May 21st and July 25th. The Calverley's first Champion, Twynfields Bryden, was made up, as was Dorothy Norman's Coombelane River Worle, owned by Felicity Wilson (nee Pegler). Bill and Ivy Leedham must have been pleased when Ivywill Wagga Wagga of Colom was made up. The Oldwell kennels collected quite a number of the CCs on offer.

In 1983 the classification at Crufts was reduced to Special Junior, Post Graduate, Limit and Open for each sex, and as a result the entry suffered. Qualification for entry was not easy as the dog had to have won a first prize at a Championship Show where CCs were on offer for the breed in either Minor Puppy, Puppy Junior, Post Graduate, Limit or Open classes, or, if it had won a first prize at Crufts the previous year, in all but Minor Puppy. Champions and dogs having won a CC or a Reserve CC the previous year also qualified for entry. Malcolm Willis, the geneticist, made a

*Ch. Lepsco Lady Elise of Flintstock JW
(Dajean Our Man Flint – Maxstoke
Meggie): Best of Breed Crufts 1992,
Bitch CC Crufts 1994, bred by Wally
Scott, owned by Janet and Alex Gunn.*

Wyburn Hannah: Winner of two CCs.

strong appeal for breeders and exhibitors to have their dogs X-rayed for hip dysplasia. He said: "In order to improve a breed, dirty washing must be done in public, but do not breed for good hips at the cost of breed type." Among the Champions, Todomas Tanya equalled her winning streak in 1981 by collecting seven CCs. Her rest in 1982 proved beneficial.

By 1984 the Kennel Club had listened to reason and we had extra classes for Puppy Dog and Bitch. The qualification was just as hard, but at least the entry was increased by fifteen dogs of which five were puppies. The new Champions shared the CCs: Jagofpeeko Inam of Oldwell and Naukeen Major Kew of Eastlynn winning five each, and Linzie of Oldwell and Naukeen Melody of Dreadnot winning four each. By this time there were 260 Champions, of which only eleven were brindles.

In 1985 the Southern Bullmastiff Society held their Golden Jubilee Championship Show with Beryl and Harris Collins as judges. Ch. Naukeen Major Kew of Eastlynn was BOB and Jagofpeeko Inara was BOS. Paignton had lost their CCs, but the Working Breeds Society of Scotland had them for the first time. By a strange coincidence, my BOB (winning his third CC) was Tartuffe Apollo to whom I had awarded the Reserve CC at Paignton eighteen months earlier. The newest Champion making a name for himself was Sharwell's Mean Mr Mustard of Pitmans. The HD scores in their present form saw Bullmastiffs included for the first time. The number of registrations was beginning to rise, from 436 in 1980 to 752 in 1985.

In 1986 an extra set of CCs was awarded and they went to the Bullmastiff Association. The judge was Margaret Reynolds and she awarded BOB to Ch. Wyburn Rula of Oldwell and BOS to Ch. Graecia Celeste. The qualification entry for Crufts 1987 eased. As well as dogs which were already Champions, the usual qualifications were extended to include second and third in both Limit and Open Classes, and any dogs which were already in the KCSB. I was the judge, and my BOB was Ch. Wyburn Rula of Oldwell and BOS was Ch. Bryany Brunette.

In 1988 Ronald James was in charge at Crufts, and the Jones's won the double. BOB was Maxstoke Gwylym and BOS was Ch. Maxstoke Bassey. For good measure we had one extra class, Special Veteran Dog or Bitch. Over the years the Craigylea affix had been allowed to lapse and this was the year in which the Galastock affix took its place. In 1988 a litter brother and sister became Champions – Galastock Danny Boy and Galastock Sugar and Spice. Galastock Sonny Boy, also from this litter, gained his title in 1991.

Crufts 1989 saw Ivy Leeham officiating, and she made Saturn of Graecia BOB and Maxstoke Elkie BOS – a first CC for both. CCs were on offer at Paignton once again. Two new names among the Champions were Norwegian Wood of Rodekes and

Ch. Bulstaff Achilles (Ch. Bulstaff Brobdingnag – Ch. Bulstaff Ambassadress of Buttonoak), owned and bred by Ruth and Ralph Short. The British breed record holder with 24 CCs.

Bostrom Amanda's Dream. By the end of 1989, there were 305 Champions and the number of brindles had risen to fifteen. February 11th 1990 was to be the last day on which Crufts was held in London. We had an increased entry, but still only eight classes. Ellis Hulme made Ch. Maxstoke Elkie BOB and Ch. Norwegian Wood of Rodekes BOS. Elkie finished up in the final six in the Working Group, but a more recent Champion, Oldwell Saxon of Bournevalley, topped this at Birmingham City when he won the Working Group. In June, Daphne Pegler awarded the third CC to Twynfields Eleazar, thus making him into a Champion. Believe it or not, he was almost ten and a half years old, but his movement put many much younger dogs to shame. The Welsh and West of England Bullmastiff Society achieved Championship status, so there were 28 sets of CCs on offer.

1991 was the centenary year of Crufts and the show was staged at the National Exhibition Centre, Birmingham. Bullmastiffs were exhibited on the first day and our ring was honoured with a visit from HRH Prince Michael of Kent. Joyce James was the judge and she awarded BOB to Rodekes Penny Lane of Penluso and BOS was Ch. Oldwell Saxon of Bournevalley. From eight classes in 1990, we went to thirteen: separate classes for Special Puppy, Special Junior, Post Graduate, Mid Limit, Limit and Open and a mixed Veteran Class. Once again, there were no CCs at Paignton. New affixes came in with the Champions Ch. Sylou Startrekker, Ch. Careless Whisper of Meitza and Ch. Beltarn Simba at Zarrott. By the end of the year ,1,064 dogs had been registered; there were 323 Champions and of these 17 were brindles.

In 1992 the Kennel Club gave the breed separate Veteran Classes at Crufts but there were only four entries altogether. Dorren Blount was the judge and her BOB carried two new affixes in Lepsco Lady Elise of Flintstock. BOS was Maxstoke Tegwyn. During the year two new Championship shows were added to the circuit – Windsor and Darlington. The Kennel Club made it harder for Bullmastiffs to gain a KCSB number. Dogs now had to win a first, second or third place in Open Classes, a first in the Limit Class, a CC or a Reserve CC at a Championship Show. We had 20 sets of CCs again and four new affixes came up among the Champions – Ch. Susamo Lucifer, Ch. Tyeoni Kiss The Bride, Ch. Dasean Golddust The Poachersfoe and Ch. Morvern Elyse. During the year Golddust won seven CCs, five with BOB.

A new change of rules for entry at Crufts in 1993 was a cruel blow to puppies. A dog under nine months of age on December 31st 1992 was not eligible for entry at Crufts in 1993 unless it had qualified for entry in the KCSB. (A dog so qualified which was between six and nine months was not eligible for entry in Special Puppy or Special Junior.) Needless to say, there were only five dogs and four bitches entered. Mary Cox found her BOB in Dajean Red Dragon and BOS in Raflyn Sweet Savanna. They were both reds, and both became Champions before the year was out. Julie Jones imported a bitch from America, who as Blazins Jubullation of Jobull (Am. imp.) she became a Champion. This must have been a good year for new affixes as among the new Champions we had Filand Man Of Harlech At Cadenham, Murbisa The Ferryman and Murbisa Spring Tides at Rossir. To round off the year Fran Harris was the judge at the LKA on December 17th. Her BOB was Ch. Dajean Red Dragon who went on to win the Working Group. The CCs were taken away from Leicester Championship Show.

Bill Newton judged at Crufts in 1994. BOB was Ch. Oldwell Trumps and BOS Ch. Lepsco Lady Elise of Flinstock. Sad to say, there was only one entry in Special Puppy Dog and two in Special Puppy Bitch, but in Special Veteran there were seven and four entries respectively. Of these, the dog, Dajean Solid As A Rock, brought a terrific round of applause from the crowded ringside. Leicester was still without CCs, but the Northern Bullmastiff Society was allocated CCs for the first time and Jack Shashtid (USA) came over to judge the show. His BOB went to Ch. Cadenham Blonde Ambition, with Ch. Jamemos Pay Homage to Carl BOS. Ch. Cadenham Blonde Ambition was taken to US by her owners in 1995 and she collected her American title. The 28 sets of CCs were well spread, and among the new Champions there was Rakwana Oberon Of Tartuffe, Brinscall Barnaby and Iron Bru Of Evenstar. Registrations rose to one 1,524.

And so to 1995 and, once again, the puppies were thin on the ground at Crufts with just two dogs and five bitches. The judge, John Campbell, made Copperfield Capt Bailey BOB, with Ch. Dajean Golddust The Poachersfoe BOS. Todomas Yvonne was the last brindle Champion in 1991, the seventeenth in line. Of the ten new Champions made up in 1995 three were brindles – Copperfield Capt Bailey, Voncalin Night Moves and Hurry Vom Frankental Of Jobull (imp. Ger.). The German import was the last Champion of the year gaining his third CC at LKA under Douglas B Oliff. The first Champion in the breed was a brindle and the last Champion of 1995 was also a brindle, making 20 brindles from a total of 363 Champions.

Up to the time of writing, in 1995, the dog winning most CCs was Ch. Bulstaff Achilles, bred and owned by Ruth and Ralph Short. He won twenty-four CCs and all but one with BoB. He was by Ch. Bulstaff Brobdingnag ex Bulstaff Ambassadress of Buttonoak. The bitch winning the most CCs is Ch. Dajean Golddust the Poachersfoe, bred by Shelley Tomsett (nee Woods) and owned by Ged and Jacqui Ling. To date, she has won twenty-one CCs and she is by Ch. Saturn of Graecia ex Dajean Golden Autocrat.

Chapter Ten

THE BULLMASTIFF WORLDWIDE

AUSTRALIA

The Early Years by John Russell, Mastodon Kennels.

Back in 1949, a Mr Ewing came to Australia from England, bringing with him a Bullmastiff pet named Major, bred by a Mr King. He was a thin-boned dog, but otherwise one that could attract and hold the interest of anyone who liked dogs. We determined that this would be the breed for us when we were ready to change from English and Irish Setters. At that time, we had the BIS Winner, Irish Setter bitch, granddaughter of the Int. Ch. Marksman of Ide, but the Bullmastiff seemed to be the answer to our search for a guard dog.

Aust. Ch. Boomerang of Bulmas: This UK import had a major influence on the breed in Australia.

Aust. Ch. Nightbeauty Benson Lee, bred by R. & M.G. Hemming, owned by the Bullmaster kennel.

Photo: D. Robinson.

Aust. Ch. Nightwatch Lady Nikita, bred by Nightwatch Bullmastiffs, owned by the Bullmaster kennel.

Photo: Animal Pics.

In 1954, we obtained from Cyril Leeke two outstanding puppies from which we started our breeding programme – Boomerang and Bush Lass of Bulmas. In January 1955 these were followed by Bonzer and Bullimby of Bulmas. Our breeding programme was started with these four and all the Bullmastiffs in Australia bearing the prefixes Mastodon, Bisonte and Behemoth are descendants from them. From a mating between Boomerang and Bush Lass of Bulmas, the first Bullmastiff puppies whelped in Australia were born on June 4th 1955. All in all, Boomerang sired eight champions, Bush Lass whelped four and Bullimby three. The first-born puppy, Mastodon the Mighty, is the sire of twelve champions to date. Boomerang and Bush Lass became the first Australian champions. The Australian climate is good for Bullmastiffs as it never gets very cold and the heat is seldom unbearable. Boomerang lived to be eight years old, Bush Lass nine and Bullimby thirteen. In 1966, Mr and Mrs Brice Lummis imported Bulstaff Maid Marian from England – in my opinion one of the finest bitches in Australia (Eng. Ch. Bulstaff Achilles ex Imogen of Vorsodene). From a mating with Behemoth Count, Marion produced Bisonte Gay Caballero who became a champion in eighteen months.

*Aust. Ch. Bulconan Apache Queen, owned
by L. & V. Cleghorn.*

*Aust. Ch. Cambalup Excalibar, owned and
bred by D. & D. Grimshaw.
Photo: Animal Pics.*

The following contribution came from *Barbara Wright, Bullmaster Kennels,* established in 1970.

The first importations for showing and breeding purposes were by Mr Jack Russell. Later breeders imported stock from Buttonoak, Bulstaff, Oldwell, Kelwall, Woodhaven and Goodstock bloodlines. The breed flourished to a peak of numbers showing in 1962, when numbers slowly fell off due to litters appearing only occasionally. Over the last two years the number of puppies produced has again increased and the future of the breed looks very bright. The Bullmastiff Club of Victoria was formed in 1964 and held its first Open Parade in 1972. A cutting from the KCC Kennel Gazette, November 1956 gives the judge's critique on the Royal Melbourne Show, 1956. "Bullmastiffs: KCC Ch. Boomerang of Bulmas (imp) received the points through his great head and expression, sound movement and bone, while the bitch KCC Ch. Bush Lass of Bulmas (imp) repeated this for the same reason. Both are massive and with grand chest width and depth. Mr Vernon Hirst." Mrs Wright states: "To follow on from Jack Russell and the Mastodon prefix, other prominent prefixes began to emerge who all played significant roles in the breeding programme of the Bullmastiff. These prefixes were:– Bisonte (Brice Lummis), Behemoth (George Fortune),

*Aust. Ch.
Bulwaren
Bergerac, bred
by E. & R. Van
Blommestein,
owned by L. &
V. Cleghorn.*

Masterville (Joy Stevenson), Bullbart (Emile Bartosy), Nairobie (Ian Wade), Harliz (Nancy Laker). From the last three mentioned prefixes emerged the Nightwatch, Wideacres and Bullmaster Kennels and they went on to be the only kennels for a number of years in Australia that were breeding. It may be of interest to note that, apart from Harliz and Nightwatch Kennels, all the others were located in one state of Australia, namely Victoria. Joy Stevenson, Brice Lummis and myself are all Life Members of the Bullmastiff Club of Victoria, Inc., the longest running club in Australia for Bullmastiffs. It was formed in 1964."

NEW ZEALAND

EARLY BULLMASTIFF IMPORTS INTO NEW ZEALAND
By Christine Powley, Arapeti Bullmastiffs.
When looking back through the New Zealand Kennel Club's archives I found the following entry: Bullmastiff: Caeser, dog, (Timber–Lassie), whelped August 1st 1948, bred by Mr S. Lowes, owned by Mr J. Pratt, Greymouth. As yet I have been unable to find out any more information on this dog. The next two were imported from Australia. They were Behemoth Crusader, fawn dog, (Mastodon Mighty–Aust. Ch. Bulstaff Delilah of Buttonoak UK imp.), whelped May 1st 1960, bred by Mr and Mrs Fortune, and Ch. Behemoth Regal Duchess, fawn bitch, (Behemoth Buccaneer–Aust. Ch. Bulstaff Delilah of Buttonoak UK imp.), whelped September 25th 1961, bred by Mr and Mrs Fortune. These two were mated together without success. Ch. Behemoth Regal Duchess was the first NZ Champion. She also did obedience training up to test B – and all

*N.Z. Ch.
Bulwaren
September
Morn, owned by
the Guardall
kennel.*

commands were given in Maori. Also imported from Australia were Wideacres Nero and Rebel Rouser, bred by Mr T. Merritt.

In 1970, Warren Hubber was in Edinburgh representing NZ in the Commonwealth Games. He saw a Bullmastiff and was so attracted to the breed that he ordered two. These were Knightguard MacGregor, red dog, (Eng. Ch. Showell Yibor–Showell Talina) whelped October 2nd 1971, bred by Mrs J. McKnight; and Minnoch of Minnyhive, red bitch, (Eng. Ch. Showell Yibor–Showell Xender) whelped November 1st 1971, bred by Major A. Flattery. These two were imported from the UK in mid-1972. While he was with Warren Hubber, Knightguard MacGregor sired four litters. In the first litter there was one dog and three bitches. In the second litter there was one dog and one bitch. Both were exported to Australia. For his third litter he was mated to Blairgowie Victoria, and she produced two bitches. For the fourth litter he was mated to Wideacres Witches Brew (imp. Aust). This mating produced Champions Bobby and Honey of Arapeti. He was later transferred to Mr J. Banks but there were no more successful matings. Minnock of Minnyhive had two litters sired by Knightguard MacGregor. These produced the foundation dog and bitch for the Knightguard Kennels, NZ. Minnoch was later transferred to us, but there were no successful matings.

Then came Wideacres Pharaoh (imp. Aust), fawn dog (Bulstaff Black Prince UK imp.–Bullbart Amanda), whelped November 5th 1971, bred by Mr T. Merritt, owned by Mr C. Bradley. Although he was often shown, his Championship papers were never applied for. He was the foundation stud of the Blairgowie Kennels. The foundation bitch was Harliz Silver Princess (imp. Aust), fawn bitch (Aust. Ch. Harliz Royal Sovereign–Penny Princess UK imp.), whelped April 6th

1972, bred by Mrs N. Laker, Tasmania. Their first mating produced ten puppies and, as the bitch failed to produce any milk, all were hand-reared. From this litter came three Champions – Jason, Marquis and Princess of Blairgowie. Harliz Silver Princess produced four puppies in her second litter and three in her third but only one became a Champion, Ch. Honey of Blairgowie.

Mr and Mrs K. Tyson imported Wideacres Fighter (imp. Aust), red dog, (Aust. Ch. Harliz Royal Sovereign–Wideacres Our Yasmin). He was mated to Harliz Silver Princess, a litter was whelped on January 18th 1976 and only one puppy became a Champion, Ch. Bonza of Blairgowie. We imported Ch. Wideacres Witches Brew from Australia. She was a fawn bitch, (Wideacres Shariff–Bullmaster Desiree) whelped May 8th 1972, bred by Mr T. Merritt. She became the foundation bitch of our Arapeti Kennels, which is one of two early kennels still going today. She was shown extensively and, when mated to Knightguard MacGregor, produced Champions Bobby and Honey of Arapeti. She was mated to Bullmaster Mason, red dog (Aust. Ch. Bullbart Achilles–Nairobie Tranquility), whelped July 12th 1972, owned by Mr and Mrs Davis. This mating produced three puppies of which Big Jim of Arapeti became a Champion. Big Jim went on to win at the National Dog Show five times. Bullmaster Mason was previously mated with Ch. Honey of Arapeti and, in the resulting litter, there were four puppies, of which Ch. Arabella and Charlie were exported to Australia. Ch. Arabella of Arapeti was extensively shown, winning Victorian Bitch of the Year five times, BOB at the Royal Show, BIS at a Specialty Show and RU BIS winner. The next import from the UK was a dog, who later became a Champion. He was Copperfield Ham Peggotty, fawn, (Maverick of Oldwell–Copperfield Flora Finching) whelped January 2nd 1975, bred by Mr and Mrs G. Warren. The owners were Dr and Mrs A. Whyte who have the Mangaroa Kennels, the only other early kennel which is still surviving. This dog was extensively shown and, when he was mated to Ch. Blairgowie Marquis, she produced seven puppies. He was later mated to Copperfield Susan Clark and there were six puppies. Of these Glencora of Mangaroa became a Champion, and Miss Blink and Donald Bean of Mangaroa were exported to Australia. In 1976 Mr A. Caley imported a dog from UK. He was Bertram of Kelwall, brindle (Eng. Ch. Frederick of Kelwall–Ailsa of Kelwall), whelped February 2nd 1976, bred by Mr and Mrs W. F. Pratt. Bertram was transferred to Mr and Mrs B. Williamson and was later transferred to us. When he first came to NZ he lived with his owner on a bird reserve. Sad to say, he was fed on bird food, which was insufficient and unsuitable for a growing Bullmastiff. This proved a handicap when he was older, as it held him back in the show ring, but although his show career was short, he left his mark on the breed, as his name is still appearing on pedigrees. He lived to be twelve and a half years old. While Bertram was with Mr Caley he was mated to Blairgowie Victoria and seven puppies were produced. After he came to us he was mated to Tina of Arapeti, and three puppies were produced. Of these, Beauty of Arapeti became a Champion. Mated once again to Tina, seven puppies were produced, and of these Cheekie and Captain of Arapeti became Champions. He was mated to Anthea of Arapeti three times. The first mating produced five puppies and the second, six puppies and Faith, Fame and Fraggle of Arapeti all became Champions. The third mating produced four puppies, of which Gail of Arapeti became a Champion. Mated to Ch. Glencora of Mangaroa, three puppies were produced. Mated to Lady Flora of Mangaroa, seven puppies were produced, of which Kanturk of Opapa became a Champion. The last time he was mated to Lady Flora of Mangaroa eight puppies were produced, of which Blyth of Opapa became a Champion.

The last of the early imports was Ch. Bullmaster Ryan (imp. Aust), brindle dog (Wideacres Shariff–Nairobie Tranquility), whelped April 4th 1976, bred by Mr P. Wright, owned by Mr and Mrs J. Banks. He had a very good show career and was also a successful sire. Mated to Ch. Blairgowie Honey, six puppies were produced. Mated to Blairgowie Victoria, fifteen puppies were

NZ Ch. Fraggle
of Arapeti.

produced in two litters and one of them later became Ch. Yellowoak Royal Guard.

THE HISTORY OF THE BRINDLE BULLMASTIFF IN NEW ZEALAND
By Mrs D. M. Jobe of Abbeyblyth Kennels.

The first brindle to arrive here was Wideacres Rebel Rouser, imported from the kennels of Mr and Mrs Merritt of Victoria, Australia. Unfortunately this dog had to have his tail docked, due to an accident while in transit. He was purchased by Mr Ivonich of Auckland but was later acquired by Mr A. Coster of Thames. He was mated to a pure-bred bitch, owned by Mr and Mrs Barnett of Auckland, and a litter of brindles and reds was produced. This was the only litter sired by Wideacres Rebel Rouser, as he passed away in 1978. Twelve months later, Mr I. Berkett from Tauranga imported a brindle bitch from Mr and Mrs Merritt. This was Wideacres Tamar. Barry and Christine Powley of Shannon took out a lease on this bitch. They mated her to their own dog, NZ Ch. Bobby of Arapeti. A litter of three puppies was produced, but none of them survived.

In 1975, Mr and Mrs J. Banks of Wellington purchased a brindle dog puppy, Bullmaster Ryan. He was the first brindle ever shown in New Zealand and the first brindle to become a Champion. Ch. Bullmaster Ryan sired nine brindle puppies for the Yellowoak Kennels. The first litter, whelped on May 6th 1977, produced Huggy Bear, Royal Lad, Brindle Lass, Ebony Dream. The second litter, whelped on March 23rd 1979, produced Silver Sheen and Dark Prince. The third litter, whelped on April 6th 1980, produced Tudor Prince, Black Knight and Maid Marion. The next brindle to arrive was Bertram of Kelwall, as has been mentioned above, who was imported by Mr A. Caley from the Kelwall Kennels of Mr and Mrs W. F. Pratt in the UK. Mr Caley had one litter from Bertram of Kelwall and there were three brindles, Baghera, Bengal Tiger and Kelly. They belonged to the Mount Bruce Kennels. Like Bertram of Kelwall, Bengal Tiger was also transferred to Barry and Christine Powley, where she produced two puppies, only one of which survived. He was Ambassador of Arapeti, a brindle, whelped on July 27th 1980. He is owned by A. Coaster of Thames and he is still alive. The Powleys produced some brindle Champions, the first of which was Ch. Beauty of Arapeti, whelped on March 12th 1983. She was followed by Ch. Captain of Arapeti, whelped on November 24th 1984; Champions Fame and Hero of Arapeti, whelped on April 27th 1986; Ch. Fraggle of Arapeti, whelped on December 23rd 1986, and Ch.

Gail of Arapeti, whelped on April 12th 1987.

Outside the Arapeti Kennels, Bertram sired twelve brindle puppies, but only one of them became a Champion. She was Ch. Blyth of Opapa from the Opapa Kennels, whelped on September 7th 1985. I was very proud to own Chs. Blyth of Opapa and Fame of Arapeti. Only one puppy survived from Blyth's first litter, Ameribelle of Abbeyblyth, whelped on November 13th 1985. The next litter, whelped on June 3rd 1986, produced five brindles – Kilroy, Kojak, Kermit, Kalimar and Kola of Abbeyblyth. The third litter, whelped on May 8th 1988, produced three brindles – Lena, Lovey and Lordlex of Abbeyblyth. Lordlex of Abbeyblyth became a Champion on May 19th 1990. He has sired two brindle puppies in my own kennels – Pirihana and Protector of Abbeyblyth, whelped on January 6th 1991 – and he has also sired five brindle puppies to outside kennels. Ch. Fame of Arapeti was a beautiful, well-boned bitch. Unfortunately she produced no puppies and died young. Other brindles which became Champions are Syra of Bullma, Blacksmear Chancellor, Rangatira Son of a Gun, Emma of Muttly Manor, Rangatira Santana and Saxon of Blueflash. These are correct according to the NZKC files up to September 1991.

There are a lot of old wives' tales told about brindles. It is said that they are scarce; they have different temperaments from reds and fawns; have lighter bone, long backs and bad head types. None of these tales are true. There is nothing particularly different about brindles when compared with fawns and reds, other than the fact that some people simply do not like them. Some judges would not put up a brindle if the rest of the dogs in the ring were dead! Personally, I think that there is nothing nicer than seeing a good brindle standing out amongst the plain reds and fawns.

FINLAND
By Riitta Maaniemi, Oddrock Bullmastiffs.
The Scandinavian countries are a strong bridgehead in regard to the breeding of the Bullmastiff in Europe outside Great Britain. The breeding in Scandinavia was begun in Finland and it was based entirely on British stock. The first Bullmastiffs in Finland were Buster of Bulmas, who was imported in 1955, and Bonnie Baby of Bulmas in 1956. They were the parents of the first Finnish-

Int. Nordic Ch. Bogerudmyra's Dilwara.

ABOVE: Fin. Ch. Oddrock Horrible Harald.

LEFT: European Junior Winner 91 Ch. Maffi's Macho Man (Ch. Oddrock Baron – Maffi's Daisy).

born Bullmastiff litter, which consisted of 4 males and 4 females, in Mr Aspelin's kennel "av Lillklobb" in 1957. Of this litter two bitches may be mentioned: Lotte was trained to be a guide-dog for the blind and she is said to have done well in her duty. The other bitch, Lippe, Finnish Champion and Winner 1966, produced the second Finnish-born litter of 1 male and 5 females in 1964, sired by Swedish Ch. Länsmansgårdens Don Bartolo (Bulstaff Figaro–Bulstaff Faith) in Mrs Airaksinen's kennel "Repoahon". This litter did well later in the exhibition rings; the bitches Risse and Renee became Finnish Champions, and Rina, Finnish and Nordic Champion. Their litter brother, Rex, who also became International and Nordic Champion, was the first Bullmastiff ever to be BIS in Finland's biggest international exhibition in Helsinki in April 1968.

The next imports were Donn and Donna of Kelwall (Ch. Oldwell Toby of Studbergh–Cortessa of Kelwall) and Della of Kelwall (Ch. Oldwell Toby of Studbergh–Cortella of Kelwall) who came to Finland in 1966. Donn sired five litters, of which may be mentioned the one with Ch. Rina. Caesar, Caius and Cassius of Old Burford became Finnish Champions and their sister Cassandra International and Nordic Champion and Winner 1970. Della produced a litter of 2 males and 7 females sired by Ch. Rex in 1967, and Donna also one, consisting of three bitches, sired by Ch. Cassius of Old Burford in 1969.

The year 1967 was a busy one on the Finnish Bullmastiff-scene. Thirty-one puppies were born of five litters and one more stud came from England. He was Morejoy Grandee (Morejoy Dawn Flash–Morejoy Captain's Lady). The dam of his litter of 5 males and 5 females was Ch. Repoahon Risse in 1969. Of these ten puppies, one especially made history. Ch. Repoahon Pontus sired thirteen litters amounting to eighty-three puppies, of which thirteen became Champions, either Finnish, Nordic or International. Of these Champions five came from his litter with Ch. Cassandra of Old Burford (Ch. Donn of Kelwall–Ch. Rina). Two of them, Suojan Sitting Bull and Suojan Sara-Trixie, were exported to Norway where they became the foundation of the Norwegian Bullmastiff breeding in Mrs Marit Sunde's kennel "Bogerudasen's" (later "Bogerudmyra's"). Ch. Suojan Sabrina was the dam of Suojan Sabotage, who sired the first brindle litter in Finland with

Odette of Oldwell (Othello of Oldwell–Simbec Clarissa of Oldwell) in 1977. When the 1970s are discussed one cannot forget such outstanding specimens as Ch. Gigolo (Ch. Repoahon Pontus–S. F. & N. Ch. Rosanna de Perros Leonados), the Champion of Champions, who won more BOBs than any other Finnish Bullmastiff so far and became twice BiS in the Helsinki International Exhibition, in 1974 and 1975. Ch. Cassius of Old Burford (Ch. Donn of Kelwall–Ch. Rina) sired twenty-four pups in the early 70s. In the late 70s a cooperation began between some Finnish and Norwegian breeders which, later on, proved very successful. The first Norwegian dog, Ola (Bogerudasen's Jules Robin–Bogerudasen's Dimple), came to Finland in 1977 and, after him, about twenty outstanding Norwegian Bullmastiffs found their homes in Finland. The most significant of them is Int & Nord Ch. Bogerudmyra's Lupin (Ch. Bogerundmyra's Bodoni–Christabel of Kelwall), who was imported in 1982 by the "Oddrock" Kennel. Papa Lupin died at the age of eleven after having sired more Champions than any other stud in the Northern countries, the most outstanding of which was Int & Nord Ch. Bogerudmyra's Dilwara, the Star of Stars in the whole of Scandinavia. "Rocky" was Nordic Winner for four years in a row in the 80s and won no less than ninety BOBs during his career. In addition to many other advantages, the Bogerudmyra dogs reach a remarkably old age. Ch. Bogerudmyra's Bodoni lived twelve years, his son Papa Lupin eleven, Ch. Dilwara's daughter Bogerudmyra's Helvite nine. At the present time there are two sons of Papa Lupin, Ch. Fatlady's Joona and Int & Nord Ch. Oddrock Coltrane, who are ten years old, and the whole of Helvite's first litter of seven, who are eight years old and all as fit as a fiddle.

In 1988 something very dramatic occurred. *Rabies* trotted over the Russian border to Finland, carried by some innocent foxes. The day the first ill specimen was located, the news was published in the afternoon papers, and the following morning Sweden and Norway dropped down the "iron curtain" that earlier had protected the Nordic countries against this evil which afflicts so many countries in the world. That was the end of all exchanges in dog breeding and showing between these two countries and Finland for many years to come. Since May 1994, Finnish dogs have been allowed to go to Sweden and Norway again, but only after very strict, long-lasting and expensive blood-tests and screening.

The fact that rabies invaded the territory of what had been clean and pure Finland was, of course, a great shock to everybody, but it did not take long for the dog breeders to realise that, although the old and safe contact to Sweden and Norway had been lost, all the rest of the world had in one instant turned wide open for us. Instead of going to shows to just our neighbours, the shows of all the world were open for us. Instead of being able to buy breeding stock from only these two neighbours and England, unless we wanted to get involved with four months quarantine, which was hard both to the dog and the buyer's economy, we could buy dogs wherever we wanted. Consequently, there was suddenly an invasion of European and American dogs into Finland and, with these specimens we got, naturally, not only the new bloodlines we so badly needed, but also new problems and new hereditary diseases we did not necessarily need.

In the 90s the most significant imports have come from the Tailwynde's and the Blackslate's in the US, from Colom, Tartuffe and Graecia in England, from Antoniushof in Germany, from Showman in Norway and from Castro-Castalia in Spain. This list would not be complete if one very special import from Norway was not mentioned – Ch. Putchi at Bullero's kennel, who has won the Club Specialty four times in a row, has been BOB and been placed in the Group more often than anyone can remember and been BIS in a big show in Estonia which made him Estonian Champion, too, and who has been, and will be, the father of many Finnish and Scandinavian Champions. Finnish Bullmastiffs have also been exported: a Bullberry dog to Blackslate's in America and another to Austria, a Paganetta's and a Para Bull's male to Austria; also an Oddrock bitch to Austria and another to Switzerland. Additionally three Oddrock Bullmastiffs have been exported to Norway and three Oddrocks and one Raiccu's to Spain. Quite recently there has arisen a keen interest in the breeding of Bullmastiffs in our eastern neighbour countries, Estonia and Russia, and some breeding specimens have been exported from Finland to these countries.

From 1957 to 1967 the number of Finnish-born Bullmastiffs grew to forty-five specimens (plus six imports from England) and so some Bullmastiff-owners decided to establish a club for all Bullmastiff-fanciers and lovers. They applied for full Breed Association rights in The Finnish Kennel Club and these were granted to them in 1970. By that year the number of Finnish Bullmastiffs had risen to about one hundred. The first official CC Breed Specialty was arranged in 1972, with forty-five dogs entered and Mr Burton from England judging. He was very pleased with the overall quality of our dogs. Since 1982 the Club Specialty has been arranged every year with breed specialists from England, the Continent and Finland as judges, and all the judges have shared Mr Burton's opinion on the high quality of our dogs.

The Breed Committee, consisting of five breeders and a specialist judge, is an essential part of the Association's activity. In addition to keeping the phenotype as close to the breed standard as possible and, naturally, the temperament, we pay great attention to the overall health of our dogs. Before a litter can be registered in The Finnish Kennel Club, both the parents must be X-rayed for HD and only the scores from A to D according to the FCI classification are qualified. From the beginning of 1996 the elbows must also be X-rayed. The Committee further recommends the dogs' eyes be examined before mating. The number of Bullmastiffs in Finland is about one thousand now, and is increasing rapidly all the time. I sincerely hope that we will still, in the future, proudly express our slogan, Quality before Quantity.

SWEDEN
By Kristina Vakkala of Kennel Kamek.

The Bullmastiff in Sweden has quite a short history. It has always been small in number, but well-established since the early 1970s. There were two litters registered earlier, one in 1959 and one in 1963. They originated, naturally, from English imports, but there was also some Finnish influence during a short period. Mrs I. Dovander, of Kennel Doggmas, got her first litter in 1973 out of a bitch imported from Finland, Swedish Nordic Ch. Samantha de Perros Leonadas (Swedish Finnish Ch. Repoahon Pontus–Resita de Perros Leonadas). Mrs Dovander is still going strong breeding Bullmastiffs. The second person to take up the breed with much good effect for years to come was Mrs B. Pettersson of Kennel Duralex (sadly deceased much too early). Mrs Pettersson found her start at the Oldwell Kennels, in the UK. Around 1975 she imported two dogs and three bitches. The one who had the strongest influence was Int. and Nord. Ch. Buckaan of Oldwell (Doomwatch Merriman of Oldwell–Suttonoak Countess Charlotte). Buckaan is the only Bullmastiff in Sweden to win BIS at the big Kennel Club Championship Shows both in Sweden and Finland, as well as BIS at the Swedish Bullmastiff and Mastiff Club Show.

Several of his offspring were successful show dogs. One of the first, Swed. Ch. Duralex Fawn King Bevis (dam Int. and Nord. Ch. Duralex Fawn Anna-Lisa, owner Kennel Kamek) won BIS at the Swedish Club Show three times. The last time he was awarded BIS was under the English judge, Mr Ronald James, and he was eight years old at the time. In a way, you can say that he was "before his time"; he would be a strong contender for BIS even today. Unfortunately he only left two litters and none of the puppies were used for breeding. However, several Duralex dogs and bitches, with the same background as Bevis and Buckaan, and offspring of Shadrack and Helga of Oldwell, are to be found in the pedigrees of most of the Swedish kennels of today. One of them, Swed. Ch. Duralex Fawn Faithful Lass, litter sister of Bevis, was the foundation of Kennel

*Swed. Ch. Kameks
Lilla Meggie, owned
by the Tombrims
kennel.
Photo: K. Vakkala.*

*Swed. Ch. Doggmas
Miss Rorly Roxanne,
owned by the
Magloff kennel.
Photo: J. Arvill.*

Kamek. In 1983, Mr S. Strömberg, of Kennel Marco Polo, imported Caiterlee Bruce of Colom (GB Ch. Colom Jumbo–Lombardy Ida) from the UK. Mr Strömberg also imported Bullmastiffs from the Maxstoke, Naukeen and Jagofpeeko Kennels. Most of them became Swedish Champions and were of great importance to the breadth of the stock. A good example is Swed. Ch. Marco Polos Emely (Swed. Ch. Jagofpeeko Remi–Mirabel of Colom), who, in combination with Marco Polos Dare Devil Dolphin (Para Bull Pure Jenkki–Colom Toowoomba), made the start for the new kennels of Cardax and Nicknames. In April 1995 Swed. Ch. Marco Polos Jumping Jack Flash, (Swed. N. Ch. Naukeen Aussie–Marco Polos Honest-to-Goodness) won BIS at a Championship show for Companion dogs. There were over five hundred entries.

Back to Caiterlee Bruce of Colom, who became Nordic Champion and was BIS under Mr William Harris, Bunsoro Kennels, in the UK. He had great type and bone to offer, which he passed to his daughter, Swed. Ch. Bogerudåsens Flora (dam Kameks Astrea, owned by Kennel Kamek).

Flora left eight Champions from three different sires and six of them were used for breeding. Flora also won BOB at the Club Show three times and BIS twice; once under Mrs M. Cox, Colom Kennels. It must have been a pleasant surprise for Mrs Cox to discover that Flora's sire was her own export. One of Flora's offspring is Swed. Ch. Kameks Kaiser (sire Todomas Benedict of Oldwell), and with Buckaan as great-great-great grandsire on the dam's side. He has been important to the breed in the latter years, leaving behind eight Champions with bitches from different kennels. Some of their offspring became Champions. Kaiser has passed on his very pleasant and special personality and you can usually recognise his offspring by their heads and expression. One of his sons, Kameks Swedish Legend, (dam Swed. Ch. Bunsoro Bangle), was exported to Latvia and was the very first Bullmastiff in the country. He made his show debut by winning a puppy Group under a British judge, in Moscow, Russia. About a year later, Kennel Doggmas exported a bitch puppy to the same family.

The brindle colour has always been in the minority in Sweden as elsewhere. A great brindle bitch was Swed. Ch. Doggmas Miss Rorty Roxanne (Doggmas Sir Jesse James–Auror). She was owned by Kennel Magloff and of course, she had Buckaan in her pedigree. She was a lovely brindle colour which came down from Shadrack of Oldwell. She became the start of Kennel Magloff with Mr and Mrs J. and A. Arvill. Roxanne produced four Champions out of seven puppies – two reds and two brindles. One of them, the red bitch Magloffs Mylam, owned by Kennel Magloff (sire Swed. Ch. Kameks Fantastiske Wilbur), is a Swed. N. and Int. Ch. and she herself has produced Champion offspring. Dogs and bitches with the same breeding as Roxanne have been used for breeding in Sweden, Norway, Finland and Denmark. One of them is Swed. Ch. Doggmas Miss Ruddy Reddy who is the foundation of Kennel Bar Bs, owned by Mrs B. Landerholm. Her breeding has had great success at Kennel Club Shows, although they are never used for breeding outside their own kennel in Sweden.

An English import which had great importance for Mrs Dovander of Kennel Doggmas was Douglas of Falconcraig. Mrs Dovander found him "in the middle of nowhere", living as a pet in the south of Sweden. From him she got Doggmas Sir Jesse James, who became sire to several Doggmas dogs and he also left behind both red and brindle champions. Mrs Dovander was also the first to turn to the Bunsoro Kennels, UK. In 1981 she imported semen from there, from Ch. Bombadillo of Bunsoro. This resulted in a litter of seven males. The dam was Renee of Hartlepool. One of the males, Swed. Ch. Isaac, owned by Kennel Doggmas, was used for breeding with good results, producing four Champions. Later, both Kennel Kamek and Kennel Magloff imported dogs from the Bunsoro Kennels. So far, three of them, Swed. Ch. Britannia of Bunsoro, Swed. Ch. Bunsoro Bangle and litter brother Swed. Ch. Bunsoro Bill Sykes, have had time to show their influence on the breed with good heads and bone. Kennel Magloff is the first Swedish kennel to import brindles from the Bunsoro Kennels. In later years some new kennels have started: Tombrims, Maxinice, Lötgårdens, Bullyards, Cosbys and Lassas.

There is one breed club in Sweden – Bullmastiff and Mastiff Vännerna (BMV) and the club has both Bullmastiffs and Mastiffs. It is part of the Swedish Kennel Club Organisation. It has been functioning for twenty years and has about two hundred members. In the Bullmastiff breed there are fewer than fifteen active breeders and an average of fifty puppies are registered each year. In Sweden the Bullmastiff is known as a charming member of the family. Generally, the Swedish breeders have been very successful in breeding for temperament. In the 70s there were some sharp, unpleasant temperaments, but today most Bullmastiffs are charming, sociable dogs.

The influence from the UK is still strong, both when it comes to importing dogs and to inviting judges. In 1994, BMV enjoyed having the author of this book, Lyn Pratt, to judge the annual club show. This show is the most important event in the whole year. A Kennel Club Show attracts four or five Bullmastiffs, but the BMV Show always get somewhere between fifty and seventy entries, and it is a Championship Show. The Club Show is also a social event, combined with barbecue, tug-of-war and "dog talk". Though the breed is small in number and the stock is very limited, the future seems bright for the Bullmastiff breed in Sweden. The active breeders who are attached to the club are very dedicated and, in a wider sense, all have the same goal for their work. The interest the breed gets from future Bullmastiff owners is most often coming from the "right sort" of people – people who want a very special, four-legged family member with a great personality.

GERMANY
By Herbert Siebold: translation by Rita Benner.
The Bullmastiff was known in Germany relatively early, but not well-known. Mostly "German" breeds were promoted, and not much attention was paid to "foreign" breeds. It was after the Second World War that the first Bullmastiff litter was bred in Germany, by a Mr Deuser who, unfortunately, did not continue breeding. The second Bullmastiff litter was born in 1975 at the kennel "von der Teufelsklinge" of Mr Natho. Over the years Mr Natho owned about ten Bullmastiffs and bred three litters. Due to adverse circumstances he, too, could not continue breeding. Two other breeders, who started at about the same time, were Mr Weber, who bred only one Bullmastiff litter, under the kennel name "von der Hofreite", and Mrs Barbara Lauterbach, who bred a litter under the kennel name "Watch Hills". She was an American and, soon after, went back to the States with her husband and her Bullmastiffs.

In 1973 my wife and I started looking for a suitable dog. We were living outside a small town and had just gone through a very bad experience. We did not know many breeds, but knew exactly what we wanted: we wanted "a dog for all seasons", a dog who, by his presence alone, would deter

Tycoon's Bella (Para Bull Oskari – Florin vom Antoniushof).

Jollibull's Ben-Kuddel (Bandog's Franco American – Blackslate's Winning Colors).

wrong-doers, a dog who would be unproblematical with the children, who would be quiet and not hectic, and who would be alert. We knew that we were looking for the impossible, and it took us a long time to find such a dog. By a lucky chance we got to know the kennel "von der Hofreite", and acquired our first Bullmastiff male, Ashley von der Hofreite, who at that time was about six months old. With him we had found the impossible: he was extremely good with our children, was easily house-trained and always went with us to the pub we managed at that time. He never bothered any of our guests, was alert, friendly, and an excellent companion.

Our first Bullmastiff gave us so much pleasure, that we decided to get a second one, a bitch. But this was easier said than done, as there was no Bullmastiff bitch to be had at that time either in Germany or in the neighbouring countries. We decided to look for her in England and, in the

ABOVE: Antonius ex Britannia (Gordon vom Antoniushof – Tailwynde's Christa).

TOP RIGHT: Black-Bega vom Dernbacher Reiter (Graecia Gladiator – Alyeska ex Britannia).

RIGHT: Adam-Amadeus vom Dernbacher Reiter (Tailwynde's Falco – Alyeska ex Britannia).

February of 1977, visited Crufts. We were lucky to meet Mrs Mary Cox and, luckier still, to acquire Colom Woopsie, who became the foundation bitch of our kennel "vom Antoniushof", and the first Bullmastiff bitch to influence the breed in Germany. She was equally successful as a brood bitch and as a show dog. She won every title she could win and many of her descendants became Champions. She started us off in breeding the Bullmastiff, and the Bullmastiff bitches living with us today go directly back to her through the female line. Over the years we have bred a total of twenty-three litters and hope to be active as breeders for many years to come. Now, in 1995, there are more than a dozen Bullmastiff breeders in Germany – some who only breed a litter every few years, some who breed more. Notable among today's breeders is Klaus Arnold, whose "vom Frankental" Bullmastiffs are presently the most successful at Continental Shows. The Bullmastiff is not a popular breed in Germany, either in or out of the ring. About ten years ago there were maybe six or eight Bullmastiffs entered at the big shows. In 1994, when Lyn Pratt judged the breed at our Club Show, we had an entry of over eighty, an absolute record entry, which might not be repeated in a hurry!

SPAIN

By Christina De Lima-Netto of Castro-Castalia Bullmastiffs.

Historically there is no doubt that Spain was a country, just like its neighbour Portugal, where the large "bull" breeds were very popular at a time when they were used to maul cattle, or at dog fights, or in the popular fights with other beasts. Once dog fights and dog mauling were prohibited, most of these large dogs disappeared, except perhaps the Spanish Mastiff, which was still extensively used for herding in the northern and central part of the country. It was not until 1980 that the first Bullmastiffs intended for breeding were imported from the UK. First was a bitch, Colom Hunter, who became the first Spanish Champion and was owned by Mr Dionisio Borja. Shortly afterwards came a male, Clyth Prionsa, owned by Mrs A. Ecija. A few months later there was another male, Sp. Ch. Coombelane River Stort, a grandson of UK Ch. Craigylea Sir Galahad.

The first litter bred in Spain was born in May 1980 – Sp. Ch. Colom Hunter ex Sp. Ch. Clyth Prionsa, at the Kindred of Haggard Kennels run by Dionisio Borja, who bred a total of eleven Spanish Champions in his six years of activity as a Bullmastiff breeder. When he stopped breeding in 1986, two other kennels started breeding Bullmastiffs, namely La Yosa Kennel and Numa Kennel. La Yosa Kennel bred more than Bullmastiffs. There were many other better-known breeds like German Shepherds, Dobermanns, Giant Schnauzers, Dachshunds, Cocker Spaniels, and Fox Terriers. So it cannot be said that they specialised or concentrated on our breed. They still managed to import some interesting stud dogs which have somehow set the basis for a so-called "Spanish gene pool". Such was the case with two Danish imports: Sp. Ch. Bullstiff Wexford (sire Pitmans Brown Bomber) and Sp. Ch. Bullstiff Buck (sire UK Ch. Lombardy Charlemagne). Much later, La Yosa Kennels imported another two males from abroad. They were Sp. Ch. Ja Pe Ros Nobody and Mercedes Pacher (sire Ja Pe Ros Mass). Although, with well above eighty litters produced, this kennel holds the record for breeding, very few Champions have been bred with this affix. Dr Alberto Cortés, a veterinarian from Zaragoza, imported from Jagofpeeko in the mid 80s Sp. Ch. Jagofpeeko Comux of Oldwell, the only Bullmastiff to have been BiS twice at the Club Special.

Regarding the Numa Kennel, located in southern Spain, it must be said that this kennel concentrated mainly on the import of British stock, although the results have been rather uneven. Nevertheless, its Sp. Ch. Numa Yapper Lanky (sire Sp. Ch. Jagofpeeko Comux of Oldwell) has been the only Spanish-bred Bullmastiff to become BIS in an International Championship Show in this country up to the present time. Numa Kennels also imported from the UK, in the early 90s, a brindle male, Sp. Ch. Simba of Granada, and from the US another brindle male, Syr Lucky of Toromas, who died of lymphosarcoma shortly after his arrival in Spain, having sired the first litter produced by the De Car Kennel. During the mid 80s, another small family-type kennel called Torrelabrada (now breeding Neapolitan Mastiffs) started its breeding programme with Sp. Ch. Kay Kindred of Haggard and produced some fifty puppies during its four years involvement with the breed.

We, at Castro-Castalia, imported our foundation bitch from the Oddrock Kennels in Finland – Sp. and Portuguese Ch. Oddrock Hotstuff – and started our breeding programme in 1991. Since then, and with only seven litters bred up to the present time, Castro-Castalia can claim to be the leading Bullmastiff breeder in Spain and has bred many national and international Champions, some of which have been exported. In 1992 at the World Dog Show in Valencia, Spain, twelve months old Ankara de Castro-Castalia (Sp. Port. Ch. Superbully de la Yosa–Sp. Port. Ch. Oddrock Hotstuff) was the only Spanish-bred Bullmastiff to win a class and BOB. Shortly afterwards Ankara became a Portuguese champion. Her litter mates, Aeneas and Ambar, have also been very successful in the show ring. Aeneas de Castro-Castalia was exported to Finland in 1991 and became Finnish Champion in 1994, having won the Junior Class at the Club Special one year

Sp. Port. Ch. Superbully de la Yosa, bred by J. Sastre, owned by Christina de Lima-Netto.

earlier. Ambar de Castro-Castalia was the first Spanish-bred bitch to win a CC in a French international show. Just recently, KGB de Castro-Castalia (sire Ch. Superbully de la Yosa) was exported to Argentina, and shortly after arriving in that country, participated in the Todas las Americas Dog Show in Uruguay, winning the Puppy Class. It became BOB and stayed at No. 2 in the Group at the age of eight and half months. Gorgeous Kharma de Castro-Castalia (sire Euro-Winner Oddrock de Castro-Castalia) joined KGB in Rosário two months later. Last but not least, on September 2nd 1995, Castro-Castalia produced its first brindle litter (sire Multiple Ch. Blackslates Mister Heartbreaker, dam Oddrock Sarah Vaughn). There were eight beautiful, sound healthy puppies. Now there are three dogs and three bitches growing steadily in the whelping box.

It should be indicated here that the main difference between the Castro-Castalia breeding programme and the rest of the Spanish breeders is the fact that a totally different bloodline was established. After choosing the Oddrock line, starting with Sp. Port. Ch. Oddrock Hotstuff, another bitch, Eurowinner Oddrock Taste of Honey (sire Mult. Ch. Bullero's Combo), and another male, Eurowinner Oddrock de Castro-Castalia (sire Mult. Ch. Maffi's Macho Man), were imported from Finland. They arrived in 1993 and 1994 to enhance and increase Castro-Castalia's breeding stock.

It should also be mentioned that in 1993 another kennel, Agafa l'Ase, started to breed Bullmastiffs, and also Fila Brasileiro and Dogo Argentino. This kennel, located in Barcelona, has imported several fawn and brindle bitches from the Les Orchis D'Orabel Kennels. It has also imported, from Germany, the Danish-bred male Ja Pe Ros Mass, which was used extensively in Germany for five years. Earlier this year it imported from the US Blazin's King Creole. This dog puppy was successfully shown at the World Show in Brussels where it won the Puppy Dog Class. As a result of the different breeding programmes in Spain during the last fifteen years, it can be said that the breed now has its own identity, although it has only started becoming popular since the early nineties.

FRANCE
By Anne-Marie Class.
The Bullmastiff was introduced into France in the 1950s and the breed is at present well-established in our country with about 150 puppies born annually. The French Bullmastiff owners are looking for a friendly family watchdog. A good number of breeders contributed to the development of the breed in France; therefore it is not possible to give the names of them all. The first Bullmastiffs registered in France were Beauty Billy of Tamara and Bellita of Beville, belonging to Mrs Langlais of Kennel Les Recollets du Lude. For many years the breed's evolution was performed without taking into consideration the breeding done in Britain. For that reason, there were different types of Bullmastiffs and some of them looked like Labradors with a black mask; this situation was amplified by the fact that there was a strong feeling against under-shot mouths. In the 1970s Mr and Mrs Corteys (Verts Paturages Kennel) tried to draw nearer to the UK and imported several products from Mrs Ruth Short (Bulstaff Kennel). Bulstaff Festival, a grandson of Ch. Bulstaff Achilles, produced many puppies, one of which was the famous Int. French and Lux. Ch. Indra des Verts Paturages (Igor). Later on, Mr Delval (Kennel Val Delbarre) worked in the same way with French and British strains. He produced several Champions, with nice, typical heads, but sometimes lacking in substance. His most famous dog was World Ch. Valmy du Val Delbarre. At this time Mr Bouillard from the Ker Brière Kennel, was producing a lot of dogs with substance, but they were a little bit too big for the standard. He used Rudy des Verts Parturages at stud several times and he was a big heavy dog.

In l985 Mrs Berthou (De Molassie Kennel), who was a lover of the breed, started to breed back to the British type. She crossed the Channel several times to buy dogs from the best British

Fr. Int. Belg. Lux. Ch. Edouard de Molossie.

Fr. Eur. Lux. Ch. Clovis de Molossie.

breeders (Oldwell, Copperfield). She also used an American strain (Tauralan) and she was able to obtain what she was looking for. She was rewarded for her work, as, from 1988, she has got one or two French Champions every year. The most famous dogs which she produced were Clovis de Malossie, French, European and Luxembourg Champion, and Edouard de Molossie, French, Int. Belgian and Luxembourg Champion and several times BIS.

The Club which manages the Bullmastiff and Mastiff breeds in France is called Club Francais du Bullmastiff et du Mastiff. It has the real power to take care of the two breeds and is dependent upon the SCC (the French Kennel Club). Most of the members of the committee work for about ten years, and this stability is certainly good for the breed. In order to improve the breed, the club invites British visitors and British judges for their National Breed Shows. The club is very careful with the health of the breed – HD, temperament and genetic diseases. To be a national Champion, a dog must have a character test and X-rays, plus CCs from a National Breed Show or Championship Show. Many of the Bullmastiffs which you can see in France today look like those found in the UK.

142

Chapter Eleven

THE BULLMASTIFF IN THE USA

by Virginia Rowland

When writing a history of the Bullmastiff breed in the United States, focusing particularly on the past twenty years, the most appropriate time to start is April 27th 1974 when a red fawn Bullmastiff, Ch. Chit's Grand Son, went Best in Show at the Tuscaloosa (Alabama) Kennel Club Dog Show. However, before we get to this very special win, it is really important that we have at least a superficial understanding of how the breeders, exhibitors and, especially the Bullmastiffs, from 1933 to 1974 made this possible.

THE EARLY YEARS
A review of the first fifty years of the Bullmastiff in the United States is basically a record of breed firsts. The Bullmastiff was recognized as pure-bred by the American Kennel Club as early as 1933. John W. Cross Jr. deserves most of the credit for getting the breed this approval. He was a sportsman who was a very active exhibitor, importer and breeder of Bullmastiffs in the thirties and early forties, and was the first President of the Bullmastiff Club of America (subsequently renamed the American Bullmastiff Association). He imported many of the breed, mostly from S. E. Moseley, including the first Bullmastiff registered by the AKC, a fawn bitch named Fascination of Felons Fear. In 1935 he, together with his wife, also registered the first American-bred Bullmastiff puppy, Felons Fear Forest Fawn. His best-known Bullmastiff was Jeanette of Brooklands of Felons Fear, bred in England by T. Pennington. She was the first Bullmastiff Champion in the United States and got the final points she needed for her Championship in 1936 by going Group 1 at the Longshore Southport Kennel Club show, a really extraordinary win. She later returned to England and got her Championship there as well. Another name associated with these early years is Pocantico, named after the Pocantico estate of John D. Rockefeller in Tarrytown, New York, where the gamekeepers' dogs were used for guarding the large property. In the 1930s the Pocantico prefix was used by Donald MacVicar, an employee of the Rockefellers, to register Bullmastiffs with the American Kennel Club. In the late forties John D. Rockefeller himself also used this prefix with Bullmastiff litters of which he was the breeder of record. One of the most influential stud dogs of this era was Pocantico Pathfinder. He was the sire of two record-making littermates. Pocantico Snowshoe, in 1947, was the first to get a Companion Dog (CD) degree. Her brother, Lancelot of North Castle, was the second Bullmastiff (after Ch. Jeanette of Brooklands of Felons Fear), and the first dog, to become a Champion. He earned his title in 1948 and, in 1950, won Best of Breed at the first Specialty held by the Bull Mastiff Club of America.

POCANTICO
Edith Pyle, who was married to Walter Pyle, the son of one of the gamekeepers at the Pocantico

estate, used the Pocantico prefix with her first litter – out of Pocantico Snowshoe CD – that was born in 1949. She continued to use it even after she and her husband moved to Vermont, where they have spent most of their lives. In the 1950s and 60s Bullmastiffs bred by Edith Pyle's Pocantico kennels contributed much to the development of the breed in the United States. She bred many ROM sires and dams. ROM is short for Register of Merit and is awarded by the American Bullmastiff Association to dogs who have more than six Champions (and/or CD degree holders) and bitches who have more than four Champions (or CD degree holders). Edith Pyle's bitch, Ch. Pocantico Runkles Treasure ROM, was Best of Breed at the Bull Mastiff Club of America Specialty twice, in 1959 and 1961, and in the following year her litter brother, Ch. Pocantico Runkles King, won Best of Breed at this Specialty. Edith Pyle is still a Bullmastiff owner but no longer an active breeder. She provided foundation stock to many breeders who are still involved with the breed.

IMPORTANT "FIRSTS"
In the 1940s and 50s another important Bullmastiff breeder and exhibitor was Dorothea Daniell Jenkins. She got her first Bullmastiff in 1936 when she lived in England. She later emigrated with her husband to Canada. She bred the first Bullmastiff to win US and Canadian Championship titles, and in 1951 this dog, US & Can. Ch. Robin of the Rouge, became the first Bullmastiff to win a Best in Show in North America at the Progressive Kennel Club show in Dixie, Ontario. He won Best of Breed at the Bullmastiff Club of America Specialty that same year.

Another notable Bullmastiff was Ch. Twit-Lee's Rajah ROM (8/10/52-4/2/64) bred by R. Lee Twitty and owned by Walter and Anita Weinstein. He was the first male Bullmastiff to win the Working Group at an important show (1955) and was placed in the Working Group many times. He won Best of Breed at the Bullmastiff Club of America Specialty Show three years in a row (1954 through 1958) and still holds the record for the most Best of Breeds won at the prestigious Westminster Kennel Club Show. He won Best of Breed five years in a row (1953-1958) and also got a Group 4 at the Show in 1955 (a total of four Bullmastiffs have placed in the Group at Westminster Kennel Club show). Rajah was a popular stud. His most famous offspring was Ch. Rajah's Lucknow Major ROM who, as the sire of 18 Champions, held the record as all-time top Bullmastiff producer for many years. He was owned by Ric Davis.

SCYLDOCGA
One of the most famous Bullmastiff breeders of the sixties was Mary Prescott. It has been said that if one goes far enough back in the pedigrees of the US Bullmastiffs, her Scyldocga prefix, or Edith Pyle's Pocantico prefix, will be found, except for those Bullmastiffs who were bred from British imports. Mary Prescott's kennel was located in New Jersey; and her stud dog Ch. Scyldocga Long John Silver ROM, a red, provided foundation stock for many of the present-day kennels. Adele Pfenninger of Tailwynde fame started out with three of his offspring – Scyldocga Dinah Horn Blower, Ch. Scyldocga Bairn McTavish ROM and Tailwynde's Amy of Thor's Glen ROM. Another son and daughter, Ch. Scyldocga Bairn McTavish ROM and Scyldocga Caroline Mathilde ROM went to Helma Week's Nutiket kennel in Pennsylvania. A Long John daughter, Ch. Scyldocga Yankee Ruth ROM, was the foundation bitch in Harry Bryant's Favo d'Mel kennel in Virginia; and a Long John grand-daughter, Scyldocga Bullmast Bronwyn ROM played a major role in Patricia O'Brien's Bullmast breeding program in California.

BULLMAST
For Patricia O'Brien breeding Bullmastiffs has been a lifetime avocation. She came to California

ABOVE: Am. Ch. Ballet of Bulmas (left) and Ch. Big Gun of Bulmas: Imported from the UK; became the first Champion bitch and dog on the West Coast.

RIGHT: Am. Ch. Baron of Bullast: The first American-bred Champion on the West Coast. Bred and owned by Leonard Smith.

Am. Ch. Brigadier of Bullmast ROM, bred and owned by Patricia O'Brien.

from England as a child in 1948. The family brought with them a puppy that they had purchased from English breeder Cyril Leeke, of Bulmas fame. Pat's father, Leonard Smith, subsequently imported other Bullmastiffs from the Bulmas kennel, including Ballet of Bulmas and Big Gun of Bulmas, who were the first female and male Bullmastiffs on the West Coast to become Champions. Cyril Leeke agreed that the Smiths' kennel name should be Bullmast. Today Patricia is still an active breeder and exhibitor and continues to use the Bullmast prefix.

FAVO D'MEL
Dr Harry and Beverly Bryant of Middleburg, Virginia, started in the breed in 1968. Their foundation dogs were Ch. Pocantico Worrysum Favo d'Mel ROM, known as Favo, and Ch. Scyldocga Yankee Rebel ROM. Favo was bred by Edith Pyle and was one of the top winning Bullmastiffs of his time. He went Best of Breed at the 1972 National Specialty of the American Bullmastiff Association and was the sire of eighteen Champions. The Bryants are not as active today in showing or breeding as they were in past years, but are still highly-respected for their love of the breed and their generosity in sharing their knowledge and Bullmastiff experiences with others.

THE FIRST BIS WINNERS
In the early sixties, the top winning Bullmastiff was US & Bda. Ch. Ritter's Beau, owned by J. P. Monge, who in 1962 made history for the breed when he won Best in Show at an all-breed show in Bermuda and thus became the first Bullmastiff from the United States to win a Best in Show. A year later he went Best of Breed at the National Specialty of the American Bullmastiff Association. Beau was very dog-aggressive – inside and outside the show ring – and was never used for breeding in the US. The second all-breed Best in Show winner was Ch. Rowley of

Oldwell, known as Odie. Carl and Jean Rabsey imported him and a few other Bullmastiffs from England. In 1966 Jean Rabsey was killed in an automobile accident, and all their dogs, except for Odie, were dispersed. Carl Rabsey continued to special Odie and, in 1967, he went Best in Show at an all-breed show in Nova Scotia, Canada. A year later, US & Can. Ch. Pixie's Imp of Cascade ROM, known as Igor, won a Best in Show in Canada. Igor was originally owned by his breeders, Bert and Mabel Kreutzer, and later co-owned by M. C. Kreutzer and G. C. Everett. He was the all-time top winning Bullmastiff of his time, with 82 Best of Breed wins, three Group 1s, and 32 Group placings. He was the sire of 13 Champions.

TAURALAN

After his wife's death, Carl Rabsey sold their two Champion bitches to Carol Beans in Santa Ana, California. One of them never produced a live litter; the other, Ch. Bulstaff Brunhilde, known as Bessie, had one live puppy, a bitch which Carol registered as Tauralan Hot Toddy. Toddy was the start of her Tauralan breeding program. This well-known kennel prefix is a combination of "taur", meaning bull, and "alan", a derivative of the medieval French name for Mastiff. Carol now has over 40 litters to her credit. She averages two to three litters a year. Her first homebred Champion was Tauralan Hot Toddy's daughter, Ch. Tauralan Tomboy. Although Tomboy had only one litter, her beauty, personality and outstanding breed type had tremendous influence on the goals Carol

Am. Ch. Tauralan Turkish Delight, bred and owned by Carol Beans.
Ashbey Photography.

Am. Ch. Tauralan Tomboy: Carol Beans' first homebred Champion, pictured in 1970.

Beans set for her breeding program. Tauralan has had two very important stud dogs, Ch. Tauralan Vic Torious ROM, a fawn, and his brindle son, Ch. Tauralan Hold That Tiger ROM. To the Beans family Vic was particularly special. When he was ten weeks old, he was stolen from the Beans' home. Two-and-a-half days later – at 3 a.m. – Carol's son Jamie heard barking coming from the front yard and discovered that Vic had been returned. For many years Vic was the all-time Top Producer for the breed. His record of 30 Champion get was subsequently surpassed by his grandson, Ch. Blackslate's Boston Blackie ROM.

Carol Beans has had much success and enjoyment in the show ring with her double Vic grand-daughter, Ch. Tauralan Turkish Delight, known as Zoe. She was a Group placer, owner-handled, and loved being shown even as a veteran, where she was unbeaten in the veteran classes.

THE BREAKTHROUGH
As I have mentioned, 1974 was a breakthrough year for the breed in the show ring. For the first time a Bullmastiff won a Best in Show in the United States. Because of the number of breeds competing in the Working Group – this was before the AKC split the breeds into two Groups, the Working and Herding Groups – it was very difficult to win a Group placement, much less a Group 1. The dog who won was Ch. Chit's Grand Son, a red fawn male called Sonny, owned by Earl and Liz Dunn, handled by Earl. They live in Muncie, Indiana, and have played an important role in

Am. Ch. Chit's Grand Son: The first Bullmastiff to win an all-breed Best in Show in the US. Co-owned by Earl and Liz Dunn.

Am. Ch. Trojan's Dusty Warrior: The first brindle to win a Best in Show. Co-owned by Earl and Liz Dunn.

Am. Ch. Needles'
Beau Colorado
N-N ROM:
Nationally ranked
for four
successive years.
Co-owned by Earl
and Liz Dunn.

getting the Bullmastiff recognized in the show ring. Their first show dog was Sonny's sire, Ch. Marine Gunner, who won the American Bullmastiff Association National Specialty in 1967. Earl campaigned Sonny for three years from 1972 to 1975 and, during that time, the dog won 100 Best of Breeds, 39 Group placements, one Best in Show and one Specialty Best of Breed from the veterans class. He was the top winning Bullmastiff in 1973 and 1974. Although the Dunns have owned several bitches and bred a few litters, they have preferred to own male Bullmastiffs and concentrate their activities in the show ring. Earl Dunn is the only Bullmastiff owner-handler in the United States to win (all breed) Best in Shows with four different Bullmastiffs. After the Dunns retired Sonny, Earl specialed Ch. Trojan's Dusty Warrior for two years. This Bullmastiff was the first brindle to win a Best in Show (October, 1980) and still holds the record as the all-time top winning brindle Bullmastiff. Another Best in Show winner campaigned by Earl Dunn was Ch. Needles' Beau Colorado N-N ROM who won a Best in Show in April, 1984 (the 11th Bullmastiff BIS winner), was nationally ranked for four years in a row, and was also a top producing sire. Beau's litter brother, Ch. Mister Fips N-N, owned by David and Janet Morris, was also a top producer and Best in Show winner in 1984 (the 10th overall). Fips won Best of Breed at the American Bullmastiff Association National Specialty in 1982 as well. Beau and Fips were bred by Virginia Bastiaans from Illinois, who was a successful breeder and exhibitor during the seventies and eighties. Fips was the sire of another Best in Show winner campaigned by Earl Dunn – Ch. Oaken's Solid Gold who was the twentieth Bullmastiff overall to win an all-breed Best in Show, in September 1989.

TAILWYNDE
A year after the Dunns' first BIS success, Ch. Tailwynde's Gentleman Barney, owned by Rick Watson, won Best in Show at the Schooley Mountain Kennel Club show, August 1975, and a month later was Best of Breed at the American Bullmastiff Association National Specialty.

Barney's breeder, Adele Pfenninger started breeding Bullmastiffs in 1969. At Mary Prescott's suggestion, she bred Scyldocga Dinah Horn Blower to the brindle Ch. Scyldocga Bairn McTavish ROM, known as Inky. From this mating she got Ch. Tailwynde's Gentleman Barney ROM. Adele had more success breeding her inbred Long John daughter, Ch. Tailwynde's Amy of Thor's Glen to Inky. Their first litter had thirteen puppies. The second litter had seventeen puppies and included the brindle Ch. Tailwynde's Rinky D'Ink, known as Smitty, who won Best of Breed at the American Bullmastiff Association National Specialty under breeder-judge Leonard Smith in 1977 and is still the only brindle Champion to go Best of Breed at the National Specialty. The breeding of Amy and Inky produced six ROM recipients. Smitty was not a ROM sire but he was the father of a very notable ROM recipient, Ch. Tailwynde's J. Paul Get 'Em ROM, a red. J. Paul's tightly inbred pedigree made him a prepotent sire. Among the fifteen Champions he sired were the two all-breed Best in Show winners, Ch. Mister Fips N-N ROM and Ch. Needles Beau Colorado N-N ROM.

The impact of Adele Pfenninger's breeding program has been felt not only in North America but in Europe, through the dogs Adele has sold overseas. Today Adele Pfenninger rarely shows her dogs, nevertheless, the influence of her breeding program can still be seen in the show ring. One noteworthy example is Ch. Mr U's Music Man ROM owned by Bill Underwood and David and Janet Morris. Known as Satchmo, he is a multi Best in Show winner (24th overall) and winner of Best of Breed at the 1991 National Specialty of the American Bullmastiff Association. He was sired by Ch. Tailwynde's Double Dutch. Satchmo was the number one Bullmastiff (all systems) 1990-1992 and he is perhaps best known for winning a Group 1 at the Westminster Kennel Club show in 1992.

Ch. Roleki's Sampson of Waterbury ROM was the fourth Bullmastiff to win an all-breed Best in Show in the United States (this was in 1977) and was Best of Breed at the 1979 National Specialty of the American Bullmastiff Association. He was bred for the first time at five-and-a-half years old and sired five litters. He had fourteen Champion get.

BANDOG

The first multi Best in Show winner (5th overall) was a fawn dog, Ch. Huck's Last Hurrah of Bandog ROM known as Freddie, bred by Louise Sanders and Helene Nietsch and sold at two years of age to Wayne and Jean Boyd. Wayne handled him to two Best in Show wins and to Best of Breed at the 1978 National Specialty of the American Bull Mastiff Association. Freddie was the Number 1 Bullmastiff for a couple of years. His dam, Ch. Bandog's Hard Hearted Hannah, died of bloat shortly after her puppies were delivered by caesarean section and Freddie and his littermates were raised by a Collie bitch. Freddie was extremely sweet-tempered and never had the macho-male type temperament we associate with Bullmastiff dogs; many have wondered if Freddie 'inherited' his temperament from his foster mother.

Louise had her first litter in 1969. The dam was Sanders Lady Guinivere and the sire US and Can. Ch. Rowley of Oldwell. This breeding produced Ch. Bandog's Conquering William, who was the first Champion bred by Louise Sanders and the first Bullmastiff owned by Helene (Buzzeo) Nietsch. For approximately ten years, they were partners in the Bandog bloodline. Louise lived in New York State and usually had ten to twelve dogs at her kennel; Helene lived nearby in Newtown, Connecticut, and kept three to five Bullmastiffs at any one time. They averaged two to three litters a year. Together they bred approximately seventy Champions and many top-producers and ROM recipients. The impact of the Bandog breeding program can be seen in many of today's top kennels, including Blazin (Roxanne and Tom La Paglia), Gunpowder (Morgan and Merry Johnson), Jubilee (Peter and Bodil Aczel), Sherwood (Mary Frazier), and Happy Legs (Alan

Am. Ch. Bandog's Crawdaddy Gumbo ROM: The top-winning Bullmastiff in the history of the breed with 37 all-breed Best in Show wins, 11 Specialty wins and 144 Groups 1s. Bred by Louise Sanders, Helene Nietsch, Ralph and Erin Stroup, owned by Jean and Wayne Boyd.

Photo: Rubin.

Am. Ch. Huck's Last Hurrah of Bandog ROM: The first multi all-breed Best in Show winner. Bred by Louise Sanders and Helene Nietsch, owned by Jean and Wayne Boyd.

Kalter and Chris Lezotte). Louise Sanders and Helene Nietsch co-bred their most famous dog with Ralph and Erin Stroup of Louisiana. Ch. Bandog's Crawdaddy Gumbo, known as Waldo, was selected by Helene from a litter that was raised by the Stroups in New Orleans. This flashy fawn puppy became the top-winning Bullmastiff of all time. He was sold to Wayne and Jean Boyd and together Wayne and Waldo achieved the following record: 544 Best of Breed wins, 11 Specialty wins including four BOB wins at the ABA National Specialty, 144 Group 1s, 377 total Group placements and thirty-seven all breed Best in Shows. He was the Number 1 Bullmastiff 1980-86 *Kennel Review* and *Canine Chronicle*, Number 2 all breeds *Kennel Review* 1984-85, and Number 1 Working Dog *Canine Chronicle*. He was also the sire of over 20 Champions.

In 1981 Louise Sanders moved to Florida and took most of the dogs with her as well as the Bandog prefix. She still breeds occasionally in Florida and shares the Bandog prefix now with Patty Stephens Sosa. Ironically, this prefix has become equally famous for the French Bulldogs currently being bred by Patty Sosa. After a brief transition, Helen Nietsch re-established her breeding program and took the kennel name Banstock. She currently has two Bullmastiff bitches at home, co-owns other Bullmastiffs, and averages one litter a year.

MORE BEST IN SHOW WINNERS

The second Bullmastiff to become a multi Best in Show Winner (and the seventh overall) was Ch. Seminole's Lone Warrior, known as Tony. He won his two Best in Shows in 1979 and 1981, handled by Joe Napolitano. Tony was a red dog, co-owned by Austin and Carolyn Boleman. Carolyn Boleman is still an active breeder. Today she lives with her nephew Keith Murray in Madison, Florida, and together they have bred or co-owned a number of ROM Bullmastiff and Champions whose pedigrees go back to breeding stock from Pocantico, Scyldocga, Tauralan and Favo d'Mel that was introduced to the Seminole line over the years.

The eighth Bullmastiff to go Best in Show in the United States – in September, 1980 – was Ch. Ladybug Staff Sargent ROM, known as Striper, who was bred by Geraldine Roach. She sold him when he was ten months old to Marilyn and Sam Dollin in Ohio. Striper won the National Specialty of the American Bullmastiff Association two years in a row, in 1980 and 1981. The Dollins bred Bullmastiffs using the kennel prefix Arborcrest during the seventies and eighties. Their most successful breeding, a Striper daughter bred to Ch. Roleki's Sampson of Waterbury

Am. Ch. Seminole Lone Warrior: A multi Best in Show winner, bred and owned by Dr Austin and Carolyn Boleman.

Am. Ch. Ladybug Staff Sargent ROM: Winner of the ABA National Specialty in 1980 and 1981. Bred by Geraldine Roach, owned by Marilyn and Sam Dollin.

Photo: Graham.

ROM, produced a total of 5 Champions and included two Group winning litter sisters, Ch. Arborcrest Touch Not the Cat ROM and Ch. Arborcrest A Ray of Sunshine ROM, and a ROM litterbrother, Ch. Arborcrest Raise the Flag ROM.

LADYBUG

The Ladybug prefix of Geraldine Roach belongs to one of the best known breeding programs in the United States. Ch. Ladybug Becky of Cascade CD ROM was the first Bullmastiff owned by Geraldine Roach. She bought her in 1969 from the Kreutzers (Cascade). Becky was a daughter of Ch. Pixie's Imp of Cascade ROM. The second bitch Gerry used for breeding was Bakerstreet Stolen Jewel ROM, known as Julie, whom she bought five years later. Julie was the dam of Ch. Ladybug Staff Sargent ROM. Gerry has bred approximately sixty Champions. Her priority has always been to breed good bitches, because at the time she started out breeding, bitches practically never won over dogs. Today most people know Gerry Roach for the bitches she bred, in particular the ones that came from the breedings between her bitch Ch. Ladybug IM Chloe, CD ROM and

Am. Ch. Ladybug IM Angelica Rose ROM: Number One Bullmastiff in 1988 and 1989, a multiple Group and Specialty winner. Bred By Geraldine Roach and co-owned by Peggy Graham.

Am. Ch. Ladybug Caitlin TD: The top winning bitch in breed history with seven Best in Shows (all-breeds), and two Best of Breeds at the ABA National Specialty.

US & Can. Ch. Blackslate's Boston Brahmin ROM. In their first litter they had US Can. & Bda. Ch. Ladybug IM Angelica Rose ROM, originally owned by Geraldine Roach and Peggy Graham and later owned by Peggy Graham and Fred and Candy Welch. Rose was the Number 1 Bullmastiff in 1988 and 1989; she was a multiple Group and Specialty winner and was handled by Alan Levine. After her specials career ended, she became a star in the whelping box: she was bred four times and so far has produced eight Champions, including Ch. Ladybug Seastar Rosebud, who has three all-breed Best in Shows wins (19 overall). Peggy Graham lives in Michigan and now co-breeds Bullmastiffs with Fred and Candy Welch (of South Carolina) using the Grawel prefix. They are currently specialing a son of Rose, US Can. & Bda. Ch. Ladybug's Thorn of the Rose BD. He is the Number 1 Bullmastiff for 1995 and won Best of Breed at the 1995 National Specialty of the American Bullmastiff Association; he is a multiple Best in Show winner Bermuda. Thorn is also handled by Alan Levine.

The second breeding between Ch. Ladybug IM Chloe CD ROM and US & Can. Ch. Blackslate's Boston Brahmin ROM produced the all-time Top Winning Bitch in breed history. Ch. Ladybug's Caitlin TD was sold as a puppy to Denise and Ralph Borton of Kalamazoo, Michigan. Caitlin was always owner-handled by Denise. She was shown 125 times and won 96 Best of Breeds, 64 Group placements, 26 Group First, seven all breed Best in Show (18th overall) plus 2 National Specialty Best of Breeds, in 1989 and 1992, and 4 other Specialty Best of Breeds. She was nationally ranked for four consecutive years, the Number 1 Bullmastiff bitch 1989 through 1992 and the Number 2 Bullmastiff in 1991 and 1992.

The third breeding between Brahmin and Chloe produced the first bitch to win a Best in Show: Ch. Ladybug's Seastar Gem (17th overall). She is owned by Jill and Stanley Cohen. Gem went Best in Show at 17 months of age and is the youngest Bullmastiff to go BIS in the United States.

Geraldine Roach started her breeding program in Pittsburgh, Pennsylvania. She later moved to Indian Mills, New Jersey, and then to Philadelphia, PA. She now lives in San Antonio, Texas, and co-owns some Bullmastiffs with Jack Shastid, who has been a Bullmastiff breeder and exhibitor for at least as many years as Gerry, using the Shastid Freehold kennel name. Ladybug and Shastid Freehold combined have bred over one hundred Champions. Gerry Roach and Jack Shastid are both licensed by the AKC to judge Bullmastiffs – as well as other working breeds – and are popular judges in the United States and overseas.

JACK SHASTID AND TAUN BROOKS

Jack Shastid started out breeding Bullmastiffs in California. He and his then wife, Taun, bred a number of Champions and imported dogs from England. US & Can. Ch. Shastid's Beefeater Phred CD, co-owned with Jim Bowers, was a Best in Show winner in Canada. Phred's sire was Ch. Securus Erebus, whom Jack imported to bring brindle genes from a different source. Erebus was the Top (Bullmastiff) Sire in 1978. After Jack and Taun Shastid divorced, he moved to Oklahoma and from there to Texas. Taun, now Taun Brooks, currently resides in Yucca Valley, California, and uses the prefix Wild Heart. One of her early successes was with a dog she co-owned with Jack Shastid, Ch. Big Sur of Bull Brook ROM; he was a consistent Group placer and an influential sire. Taun Brooks is a truly talented Bullmastiff handler. She has shown innumerable dogs to their Championship for herself and other breeders; she has campaigned a number of Bullmastiffs successfully, including Ch. Wild Heart's Sampson ROM, a red fawn male she bred and later co-owned with M. Soeten, who was an all-breed Best in Show winner (14th overall) and an important sire on the West Coast.

BLACKSLATE

The Blackslate breeding program of Virginia Rowland and Mary B. Walsh had similar beginnings to some of the other breeding programs that began in the late sixties. Their foundation bitch, Ch. Bullstar Blackslate's Hecuba ROM, was a granddaughter of Bulstaff Black Magic, a brindle male imported by the Rabseys, whom Carl Rabsey gave to his father-in-law in Massachusetts after Jean's death, and Katrina of Cascade, a full sister of Ch. Ladybug Becky of Cascade CD. Blackslate's first litter was whelped in 1974 and since then this breeding program has produced many Champions and top producers. US Int. and Span. Ch. Blackslate's Boston Blackie ROM, known as Mister, a brindle son of Ch. Tauralan Hold That Tiger ROM, still holds the record as the all-time top producing Bullmastiff in the United States; he is the sire of 41 US Champions. Mister was shown briefly in Spain and Portugal and became the first Bullmastiff to win a Best in Show in both these countries. His son, US and Can. Ch. Blackslate's Boston Brahmin ROM, a red male co-owned with Dolores Merlino, excelled equally as a sire and as a show dog. He is a multiple Best in Show winner (16th overall) and the sire of 40 US Champions including two Best in Show winning daughters and two Best in Show winning sons. His son, Int. Ch. Bullberry Ghostbuster, won a Best in Show in Austria. Ch. Leatherneck Grizzly, another Brahmin son, went Best in Show in October 1995 (29th overall). One of the all-time favorites at Blackslate was Ch. Sunny Brook's Sweet Sarah, a stud service puppy sired by Ch. Blackslate's Big Daddy Henry ROM. Sarah was the first bitch in 25 years to win Best of Breed at the National Specialty of the American Bullmastiff Association in 1986 and was the first bitch in 50 years to win Best of Breed at the Westminster Kennel Club show. She was the Number One Bullmastiff Routledge system (breed points), an award that a Bullmastiff bitch had never achieved. Her success in the show ring helped pave the way for her grand-nieces, US & Can. Ch. Ladybug IM Anglice Rose and Ch. Ladybug Caitlin TD.

Blackslate has sold puppies to many countries in Europe and today the grand-children and great-grand-children of Mister and Brahmin are excelling in show rings in Germany, Austria, Belgium, Spain and Scandinavia as well as the United States and Canada. There are more ROM recipients with the kennel prefix Blackslate than any other kennel in the United States. Mister's and Brahmin's ROM get have made significant contributions to other breeding programs. Mister's ROM sons include: Ch. Blackslate's Duke of Sandcastle, owned by Sheila Hineline and Vicki Kotrba (Sandcastle), sire of twenty-plus Champions; Ch. Allstar Terry Thomas, owned by Mimi Einstein; litter brothers Ch. Blackslate's Action Jackson, owned by Lisa Lane (Zildjian) and Blackslate Kennels, and Kastle Jennat's Barberic Obsession, owned by Eric Long and Barbara Moffat (Barberic). Mister has two sons in Europe who have been successful sires – Int. Ch. Blackslate's Mister Heartbreaker, owned by Tommy Stenberg and Ragnhild Folkestad in Norway, and Int. Ch. Blackslate's Boston Diplomat, owned by Christine Cappelle in Belgium. Brahmin's ROM sons include Ch. DOX Fast Freddy of Shady Oak and Ch. Leatherneck Grizzly.

BLAZIN'
Another well-known kennel is Tom and Roxanne LaPaglia's Blazin' Bullmastiffs. The LaPaglias live in Churchville, Maryland. Their foundation Bullmastiffs were Ch. Dalstock Fancy Fanny ROM, a brindle, and Stonykill Red Devil Dunnit ROM, a red, from which they bred one of their most famous sires and show dogs, Ch. Blazin's Brahma Bull ROM. Between 1982 and 1987, Fanny had a total of five litters and produced thirteen Champions. The LaPaglias have bred many Champions and ROM producers. Ch. Blazin's Hurricane Barklay, a red fawn male they sold to Kay Siebert and Patrick O. Gudridge, was a Best in Show winner in Canada in 1991 and was nationally ranked. Ch. Blazin's Panzer, owned by Melinda Raby and Peter Kozel, was Best of Breed at the 1994 National Specialty of the American Bullmastiff Association, under breeder-judge Geraldine Roach. The LaPaglias are currently campaigning a son of Brahma, Ch. Blazin's Blue Max, that they co-own with Greg Slater. Max has been nationally ranked in 1994 and 1995 and is a multiple Group winner. In 1992 the LaPaglias sold a bitch to Julie Jones in England. Eng. Ch. Blazin's Jubullation of Jobull became the first bitch after Ch. Jeanette of Brooklands of Felons Fear to go from the United States to England and become an English Champion.

THE TOP PRODUCING BITCH
The Bullmastiff bitch who still holds the record as the all-time Top Producer in breed history in the United States was a brindle, Ch. Fairview's Roxanne By Guv ROM. She was bred by the late Marti Robins and was co-owned by Vic Zeoli. In her first litter, born in 1982, she free-whelped twelve puppies, ten of which became Champions. Roxy has a total of four litters and in all has had 15 Champion get.

MORE KENNELS OF TODAY
A merger of two successful Bullmastiff breeders and exhibitors occurred in 1994 when Terry Gaskins and Dean Aamodt married. They brought with them the offspring of two established breeding programs. Dean and Terry both started out in California. Dean got his first Bullmastiff in 1977 as a teenager. He co-owned his first show dog with his mother, Claudette. US Can. Mex. & Int. Ch. Little Caesar ROM, known as Gus, accumulated over 250 Best of Breed wins, numerous Group placements and two regional Specialty wins. Ch. Aamodt's Little Cyrus Noble ROM finished his Championship at nine-and-a-half months of age and was a multi Group winner and placer. In 1989 he became the first Bullmastiff to win a Best Show in California (22 overall). He lived with three other adult Bullmastiff males without one aggressive incident. All told, 18 litters have borne the Aamodt prefix, with twelve puppies becoming Champions. Terry (Gaskins) Aamodt acquired her first Bullmastiff in 1983. Her first real success with a Bullmastiff in the show ring was with US Mex. Int. Ch. Tauralan Triga de Azteca ROM. Terry bought Triga in 1984 and

Am. Ch. Fairview's Roxanne By Guv ROM: The top producer in the breed with 15 Champion offspring. Bred by Marti Robins and co-owned with Vic Zeoli.

handled her to Best in Sweepstakes at the American Bullmastiff Association National Specialty that year. Triga had many Best of Breed wins, most memorable being Best of Breed at the ABA Far West Specialty in 1986. Prior to her marriage, Terry's kennel name was Upper Crust. She has shown a number of Bullmastiffs to their Championship and her greatest success so far has come with US Mex. and Int. Ch. Upper Crust Weekend Warrior, known as Genghis. He had over 30 Group placements and won the ABA Far West Specialty two years in a row, 1991 and 1992. In 1992 he went Best in Show in Las Vegas, Nevada (23rd Bullmastiff overall). Gus, Cyrus and Genghis were grandfather, father and son. All three were nationally ranked and Cyrus and Genghis were the second Bullmastiff father and son to go Best in Show in the United States. Dean and Terry Aamodt and Claudette Aamodt currently reside in Bailey, North Carolina.

There are now a number of successful show kennels whose achievements should be acknowledged. Dr and Mrs John Crawford of Oak Park, Illinois, have one of the largest. They started with two litter sisters they co-owned with Pam Kochuba, sired by Ch. Arborcrest Raise the Flag ROM: Ch. Shady Oak's Subtle Sylvia ROM and Ch. Shady Oak's Great Grr-Annie CD ROM. Annie's breeding to Ch. Shatrugo's Jonathan Q. Higgins produced five Champion get. Sylvia was bred to Ch. Blackslate's Barton Brahmin three times and there were six Champions produced. The first litter included US, Chilean, S. Amer. Ch. Amers. 89, Int. CPHN, World 89, Bah. Can. Ch. DOX Fast Freddy of Shady Oak ROM, known as Fred. He holds the record for the most Championship titles earned by a Bullmastiff. Prior to Fred's recent retirement as a stud dog, the DOX breeding program revolved around him, his get and his grand-kids. With thirty-nine Champion get so far, he is guaranteed to break the record of his sire, Ch. Blackslate's Boston Brahmin. A fawn daughter of Fred's litter sister (Ch. DOX I Potato II of Shady Oak), US & Can. Ch. Shady Oak DOX Fetching Frieda, is a multi Best in Show winner in the United States (27th overall) and Canada, and has been nationally ranked in the United States from 1993 to 1995. Before the Crawfords started specialing Frieda in the United States, she was shown in Canada and was the Number 1 Bullmastiff there.

Another successful kennel in the Midwest is the Happy Legs kennel of Chris Lezotte and Alan Kalter, based in Ann Arbor, Michigan. Their breeding program began as a combination of two

*Am. Ch. Aamodt's Little Cyrus Noble
ROM: The first Bullmastiff to win an all-
breed Best in Show in California. Bred and
owned by Dean and Claudette Aamodt.*

*Am. Mex. Int. Ch. Upper Crust's Weekend
Warrior: An all-breed Best in Show winner
in 1992, and winner of the Far West ABA
Specialty in 1991 and 1992.*

*Am. Chilean, S. Am.
Ch. Amers 89, Int.
CPHN, World 89,
Bah. Can. Ch. DOX
Fast Freddy of
Shady Oak ROM,
breed and owned by
Dr John and Susan
Crawford and Pam
Kochuba.*

ABOVE: Am. Ch. Jubilee Willie's Legacy, owned by Peter and Bodil Aczel.

TOP RIGHT: Am. Ch. Happy Legs Luke of Hartford: Nationally ranked 1992 and 1993. Bred by Chris Lezotte and Alan Kalter.

Ashbey Photography.

RIGHT: Am. Can. Ch. Shastid Beefeater Phred CD: Nationally ranked, and an all-breed Best in Show winner in Canada. Co-owned by Jack Shastid and Jim Bowers.

successful Eastern kennels: Bandog and Jubilee (Peter and Bodil Aczel). They had their first litter in 1986 and finished their first homebred Champion in 1989. They have bred or owned forty-four Champions: these include Group and Specialty winners, top producers and ROM recipients. Their fawn male, Ch. Leatherneck Bit of Happy Legs, was the youngest Bullmastiff male in the history of the breed to win an all-breed Best in Show (27th overall) at twenty months of age.

The Leatherneck Bullmastiffs of Anita Lewis (Brentwood, Tennessee) and Jean Robinson (Frankfurt, Indiana) is another breeding program that has produced many Specialty winners, Champions and ROM recipients. Another successful breeding program belongs to Dr Dwayne and Judy Nash. The Nashs live in Stockton, California. They are currently showing their third generation of Specialty-winning Ramsgate Bullmastiffs. Jerry and Marjorie Tackett of Little Rock, Arkansas, have been breeding and exhibiting Bullmastiffs for over fifteen years. They use the prefix "J-Mar". Jerry Tackett is one of the talented Bullmastiff owner-handlers.

Mimi Einstein's Allstar Bullmastiffs of Katonah, New York, have also excelled in the show ring. Her two ROM sires, Allstar's Pal Joey ROM, a red son of Ch. Blazin's Brahma Bull ROM and

Mimi's foundation bitch Ch. Tailwynde's Kiss Me Kate, and Ch. Allstar's Terry Thomas ROM, a brindle son of Ch. Blackslate's Boston Blackie ROM, have contributed mightily to the success of her breeding program. Joey's son, Ch. Allstar's Martin Riggs, was the twenty-first Bullmastiff overall to win an all-breed Best in Show. Martin Riggs' litter sister, Ch. Allstar's Hawks Flight KOA, was bred to Terry Thomas and produced Ch. Allstar's Mugsy Malone, a multiple Best in Show winner (25th overall) who is owned by Ken and Debbie Vargas.

BULLMASTIFFS AND OBEDIENCE

Bullmastiffs have not excelled to anywhere near the same degree in the Obedience ring as they have in breed competition. Their special brand of intelligence and independent thinking does not lend itself to the type of training that would produce an AKC Obedience Champion. As of 1994, there have never been more than eighteen Bullmastiffs to get their CD titles in one year (1989). The first Bullmastiff to earn a CDX (Companion Dog Excellent) degree was a bitch, Boadicea, in 1958. As of 1994 there were 30 Bullmastiffs with CDX degrees – the most earned in one year was 3 – and 9 Bullmastiffs have earned UD (Utility) degrees, the first of which was Ch. Dark Gem of Sunnyhill UD ROM in 1960. Approximately 10 Bullmastiffs have earned a TD (Tracking) degree and none have earned a TDX, the Tracking Dog Excellent degree. There are no Obedience Champions, and no Bullmastiffs have earned UDX degrees (Utility Dog Excellent).

There are a few owner/trainers who deserve much credit for their dedication to Obedience training and the success they have achieved working with their Bullmastiffs. Joel and Maryanne Duchin have been training their Bullmastiffs in Obedience since 1975. Joel is the trainer, and he has put CD titles on six Bullmastiffs that he personally owns, and has also helped to train other people's Bullmastiffs. He has trained three of his Bullmastiffs to CDX degrees and two Bullmastiffs to UD degrees; these were Lady Travis of the Bluegrass UD, known as Lady, and Ch. Watch Hill's Evita UD, known as Margo. Margo and Lady were the Number 1 and Number 2 Obedience Bullmastiffs in 1986. Margo got first place in Utility at the second largest show in the country in 1986, which was an unheard-of feat for a Bullmastiff. The Duchins live in Melbourne, Kentucky, and breed on a limited basis with the Bluegrass prefix.

Dr Rober and Lynn Spohr have been breeding Bullmastiffs, with the kennel prefix Bastion, who have excelled in Breed and Obedience. The Spohrs live in Jenks, Oklahoma. Jenny Baum (Beowulf) of Atlanta, Georgia, is a young breeder who is equally devoted to, and successful in, showing her Bullmastiffs in Breed, Obedience and Agility. Mona Lindau-Webb of Los Angeles, California, is another enthusiastic trainer who has exhibited her Bullmastiffs in Breed, Obedience and Schutzhund, and, in 1995, made breed history when her bitch, Tauralan Tequila Sunrise NA, became the first Bullmastiff to win the AKC's newly-introduced Novice Agility degree.

PROTECTING THE BULLMASTIFF

Many of the Bullmastiff owners and breeders mentioned in this chapter have contributed to the Bullmastiff's welfare in many ways. All are members of the American Bullmastiff Association, many have served as President of the ABA – Earl Dunn, Patricia O'Brien, Carol Beans, Virginia Rowland, Jack Shastid and Helene Nietsch. Mary Anne Duchin, Chris Lezotte, Marti Robins, Marjorie Tackett and Mimi Einstein have all been ABA Secretary, and Gerry Roach, Roxanne LaPaglia, Mary B. Walsh, Denise Borton and Bob Spohr have all served in other Board positions. Virtually all of them have helped as necessary with the rescue program of the ABA. Adele Pfenninger is a truly talented artist whose donations of artwork to the American Bullmastiff Association have helped keep it solvent. Carol Beans is the editor of two popular privately published breed publications, *The Bullseye* and *The Pedigree Pictorial*. Lynn Spohr is the editor of

The Register of Merit Book, which has been an invaluable resource for this chapter, as have Helma Weeks' articles and statistics published in the *Bullmastiff Bulletin*, the magazine of the American Bullmastiff Association.

REVISIONS TO THE BREED STANDARD
The official Bullmastiff Standard in the United States was most recently revised by the American Bullmastiff Association and (re)approved by the American Kennel Club in 1992. The changes were made at the request of the AKC who wanted all Breed Standards to have the same format. In addition to the format changes, a new section on 'gait' was introduced and, in the section on size, proportion and substance, a description of the Bullmastiff as "nearly square" was introduced.

LOOKING TO THE FUTURE
The Bullmastiff breed in the United States has been fortunate that it has not experienced the type of explosion in popularity that some of the other working breeds, including Rottweilers, Dobermanns and Boxers have suffered from. Nevertheless, there has been a dramatic increase in the numbers of Bullmastiff litters annually registered. In 1972 there were 140 Bullmastiff litters registered; in 1976, 200 litters; in 1980, 259 litters; in 1989, 363 litters and in 1992, 473 litters. In 1994, the last year for which statistics are available, 2373 individual Bullmastiffs and 574 litters were registered. Compare this to the figures for Rottweilers – 102,596 individual dogs and 31,147 litters. The number of new Bullmastiff Champions has increased likewise. In 1972 there were 47 new Champions; in 1976, 78 new Champions; in 1980, 78; in 1989, 118, and in 1994, 197 new Champions. In the twenty-plus years since a Bullmastiff won an all breed Best in Show in the United States for the first time, Bullmastiffs – dogs and bitches – have gotten more and more recognition at all levels of AKC breed competition. So far there have been 29 Bullmastiffs – 25 dogs and 4 bitches – Best in Show winners (at all breed shows) in the United States. Competing at a Group level in the United States is very tough, as many of the Group and Best in Show judges expect a degree of showmanship that is not a Bullmastiff breed characteristic. Most of the top show dogs are professionally handled, competing at shows sometimes 50 weekends a year. Winning at the Group level against flashier breeds such as Boxers, Dobermanns, Great Danes, Siberian Huskies and Giant Schnauzers is difficult, and it is no accident that the Bullmastiff dog and bitch who hold the record for Best in Show wins were owner-handled. Most owners do not have the time, talent, or money to compete at this level, so the records Ch. Bandog Crawdaddy Gumbo ROM and Ch. Ladybug Caitlin TD achieved should stand for many, many years.

We have a new generation of Bullmastiff breeders and exhibitors. Jenny Baum has been very successful. Lisa Lane (Zildjian), who lives in China Grove, North Carolina, has bred a number of Champions and is the proud owner of two ROM recipients. Dionne Shastid, daughter of Jack Shastid and Taun Brooks, is a marvellous handler and has handled her red fawn Ch. Wil Heart's Thunder Too to national rankings two years in a row. Connie Urbanski and Susan Borg (Whiskey Hill) live in northern California. Their fawn Ch. Whiskey Hill's Bootlegger is a recent Best in Show winner (28th overall). Charles and Zoe Murphy (Whyloway) are another young couple that are very active in the breed. Charlie has had Bullmastiffs most of his life and has been breeding and exhibiting for many years. His wife, Zoe, has given much of her time and enthusiasm to the American Bullmastiff Association. The successes of Aamodt Bullmastiffs and Terry and Dean Aamodt have already been recorded. To all these "young" breeder-exhibitors: Take care of the breed, the future is in your hands.